Livin' on Country

By Scott Gray
Published by The Ballantine Publishing Group:

Livin' on Country

The Alan Jackson Story

Scott Gray

BALLANTINE BOOKS • NEW YORK

A Ballantine Book
Published by The Ballantine Publishing Group
Copyright © 2000 by Scott Gray

All rights reserved under International and Pan-American Copyright Conventions. Published in the United States by The Ballantine Publishing Group, a division of Random House, Inc., New York, and simultaneously in Canada by Random House of Canada Limited, Toronto.

Ballantine and colophon are registered trademarks of Random House, Inc.

www.randomhouse.com/BB/

Library of Congress Catalog Card Number: 00-190528

ISBN 0-345-43873-6

Cover photo © James Schnepf/Gamma Liaison

Interior photos © Alan L. Mayor

Manufactured in the United States of America

First Edition: June 2000

10 9 8 7 6 5 4 3 2 1

Contents

Acknowledgments   vii

What the Critics Say About Alan Jackson   ix

One   Best in Class   1

Two   Southern Born   11

Three   Livin' on Love   23

Four   Dreamin' It Real   33

Five   Catchin' That Rainbow   49

Six   Hold on Tight   65

Seven   Move on Up   79

Eight   Year to Remember   91

Nine   King of Country   103

CONTENTS

Ten   Back to Basics   115

Eleven   Keepin' the Pace   131

Twelve   Stayin' Together   143

Fourteen   Pure Tradition   151

Alan On . . .   155

Appendix I   Personal Data   159

Appendix II Discography   162

Appendix III Awards and Honors   164

Acknowledgments

I tell people now when they ask me, I say,
"Do what's in your heart and don't let people
change you. Do what you want to do."
—ALAN JACKSON

Thanks foremost to Mr. Alan Jackson for the songs, the stories, and the inspirations.

The professionals at Ballantine Books—in this case Cathy Repetti, Mark Rifkin, Nancy Delia, and Caron Harris—are passionate about books. It's with utmost pleasure that I call them colleagues and friends.

I can't say enough about my parents. They offer unwavering support and ask nothing in return but that I try to honor my fellow humans and myself. If the term "good people" were in the dictionary—and it should be!—my mother and father would be pictured.

What the Critics Say About Alan Jackson

"If others have helped churn up huge new audiences, Jackson has taken care to instruct them in the basics of country tradition."
   —Gene Harbrecht, *Orange County Register*

"If the music industry gave awards for niceness, country singer Alan Jackson would have a bushel-basket full."
   —Randy Lewis, *Los Angeles Times*

"He's a country artist who's here to stay and will be well remembered in music history, and, man, the brakes aren't on yet."
   —Fish Griwkowsky, *Toronto Express*

"Another long tall Southern singer-songwriter with the stamp of red-clay ruralism on his music, Jackson is perhaps the closest thing on the country scene to a reincarnation of [Hank] Williams."
   —Jack Hurst, *Chicago Tribune*

"There have been many claimants for the mantle of Hank Williams's songwriting legacy. Alan Jackson has proven himself to be supreme amongst those claimants."

—Janet Bird, *Definitive Country: The Ultimate Encyclopedia of Country Music and Its Performers*

"What sets Jackson apart from so many of his contemporaries is talent and taste. This good ole boy from Georgia is, plain and simple, the real deal."

—David Sowd, *Akron Beacon Journal*

"Alan Jackson is one of the few remaining . . . who sing about honky-tonks and heartaches in the best George Jones tradition. . . . Whether delivering a soulful ballad . . . or a road-house romper . . . his music is always front and center."

—Jim Santella, *Buffalo News*

"A conversation with Alan Jackson is like talking with an old friend."

—Gary Leftwich, *Newnan Times-Herald*

ONE

Best in Class

> You know that song, "Who's Gonna Fill Their
> Shoes . . ."? I don't know whether I can fill 'em,
> but I'd sure like to try 'em on.
> —ALAN JACKSON

The acclaimed Class of '89 will go down as the most influential conflux of debut artists in Nashville history. That single landmark year marked the arrival of no less than five singers who would become among the most successful country artists of the 1990s: Clint Black, Garth Brooks, Mary-Chapin Carpenter, Travis Tritt, and a then-thirty-one-year-old Georgia native named Alan Eugene Jackson.

June 1989 saw Black become the first new male artist in more than a decade to score a *Billboard* No. 1 debut single ("Better Man"). Tritt and Carpenter cracked the Top 10 in September, and Brooks topped the charts in December with "If Tomorrow Never Comes." In fact, Jackson was the lone Class of '89er not to break through in a big way in 1989, as his leadoff single, "Blue Blooded

Woman," stalled before it reached the Top 40. Alan didn't have to wait too long, though, to join his peers on the upper part of the *Billboard* chart. His next release, "Here in the Real World," shot straight to No. 3 a couple of months into 1990. "That song took us from hamburgers to steaks," Alan joked at Fan Fair in 1998.

While he lagged behind the others in notching that first smash hit, Alan has since surpassed all but Brooks in total career credits. From 1990 through 1996 Alan ranked as the third-most-accomplished artist in country music, according to *Billboard*, trailing only Garthosaurous Rex and George Strait. Of course, comparisons of that sort don't mean much to Alan, who does what he does and lets the accolades fall where they may.

The success doesn't mean I can coast. But it does help you to maybe relax, concentrate more on the music, and not worry about album sales or where your album's at on the charts.

—ALAN JACKSON

Best in Class

There's no doubt that a lion's share of accolades have fallen in Alan's direction: seven Academy of Country Music Awards, seven Country Music Association trophies, and a couple dozen honors from the TNN/Music City News Awards are the fruits of his labors. What's more, Alan has been repeatedly recognized by ASCAP for his songwriting, and his certified sales exceed twenty-four million. For a decade, Alan has done his class proud and has been one of the few constants in a changing Nashville landscape.

> He's one of those people that when we get a single across our desk, there's no question we're going to end up adding it [to the playlist].
> —LISA PUZO, KZLA-FM

The Class of '89 jump-started a period of unprecedented commercial success in country music, but it also spawned a wave of artistic upheaval. The continuing melding of rock song structures and honky-tonk instrumentation, not to mention an increasing focus on marketable looks, bumped the old guard off the charts and radio playlists. It took no time for the older stars to be all but forgotten by radio programmers, executives, and the new urban fan base.

In truth, old-school hard-country sounds had been waging an uphill battle since the time the Beatles landed on American soil. Alan once pointed out in the *Minneapolis Star Tribune* that the tug-of-war is ongoing: "You've always had traditional country vs. contemporary country," he noted. Contemporary (i.e., rock) stylings can be heard in country songs at least from the time Buck Owens put a fuzz-tone guitar solo in his 1969 smash "Who's Gonna Mow Your Grass."

Throughout the 1970s, country singers from George Jones to Charlie Rich flirted (and often hopped into bed) with all kinds of pop and rock sounds. George covered pop-folkie James Taylor (not that there's anything wrong with that), and Charlie's "The Most Beautiful Girl" was a pop crossover if ever there was one. Even the so-called Outlaws (Kris Kristofferson, Waylon Jennings, et al.) had the rock-and-roll spirit—and sometimes the sound, too.

Trouble was, by the 1980s, around the time Alan hit his early twenties, the blending of forms had skewed things to the point where country was being totally absorbed by rock and pop. Take

"Islands in the Stream," as performed by Kenny Rogers and Dolly Parton and written by the Bee Gees; it may represent the biggest gap of all time between commercial success and any semblance of genre integrity. The song marked the sales apex of the Urban Cowboy era and was performed by two artists generally thought of as "country"; yet if it'd been done by Donny and Marie Osmond, it's possible nobody would've known the difference.

> But there's always been pop-country and country-rock, then it goes back to traditional country. Back and forth. It's always been that way.
> —ALAN JACKSON

According to Alan, "Back in the late '70s and early '80s, the progressive stuff dominated it all." In the 1970s the *Billboard* charts were brimming with AM-radio country that was either pop-inflected, folk-tinged, or rock-influenced—culminating in the Urban Cowboy trend of 1980. Consider that the soundtrack to *Urban Cowboy* featured songs by rockers such as Bob Seger and Joe Walsh. The emergence of the New Traditionalists—George

Strait, Ricky Skaggs, Randy Travis are the first who spring to mind—was a reminder that Nashville could get back to its roots and still sound fresh.

So the stage was set for Black, Brooks, et al. Each had grown up listening to as much rock as country, and each was inspired by the New Traditionalists. Fans welcomed the Class of '89 with open ears, but critics began to focus on the question of who among the newcomers would keep the torch lit for traditional country music. Alan Jackson was tabbed as the most promising candidate, and he would more than live up to the expectations.

> I wanted to be one of the new singers that did real country.
> —ALAN JACKSON

The opening months of 1990 featured a circumstance the likes of which won't soon be duplicated in the Atlanta music scene. A trio of new country singers, all hailing from or near the Georgia capital, had released major-label debut albums that were expected to be strong sellers. "It's just kind of bizarre that we've got three acts coming out of Georgia right now," Alan told an *Atlanta*

Journal-Constitution writer. "I don't know what caused it."

The timing was, in fact, coincidental, but the success of the newbies had nothing to do with chance. This was a case of three talented singers each deserving the hoopla surrounding his arrival. The rockin' southern outlaw Travis Tritt and the cry-in-your-beer balladeer Doug Stone were alongside Alan on the New Arrivals shelf.

Stone's first single, "I'd Be Better Off (In a Pine Box)," sailed to No. 4 on the *Billboard* chart. It was the first of fifteen top tens he would post over the next five years. Tritt's "Help Me Hold On," the follow-up to his breakthrough hit, "Country Club," was the first of the eight songs he would take to No. 2 or higher during the course of his career to date.

Nashville is a very small world, and none other than Alan Jackson had been the singer on a demonstration recording of "Country Club" (for writers Catesby Jones and Dennis Lord) two years before Tritt made the song a hit. In those days Alan toiled in the less glamorous corners of the business: writing songs, singing demos, and performing in bars. No one thought of him as a future superstar; in fact, at one point a label executive told Alan flat-out that he had no star potential.

> Things like that are hard to swallow. But a lot of times you've just got to realize that's only one man's opinion, and not let it stop you from keepin' right on trying.
> —ALAN JACKSON

In yet another Nashville twist, the song that put Alan on the public's radar screen, "Here in the Real World," was almost the debut single for another artist two years earlier. Tony Perez, a newcomer signed by Warner Bros. in 1988, recorded the song. According to Alan, "They said they loved it, and they cut it, and it was going to be his first single."

It turned out that there was a change in producers on the Perez project, and the song wound up not being used. It was sent back to Alan, who took it to No. 3 on the *Billboard* chart in February 1990. Alan had taken the opening line and a melody, collaborated with songwriter Mark Irwin for an hour or so, and come up with the song that jump-started his career.

The listener support for "Here in the Real World" translated into big orders for the album of the same name. An initial load of 200,000 copies of *Here in the Real World* was shipped to retailers, a terrific number in a time when 300,000 was considered the megahit plateau. Alan was off to a fast start, solidifying his spot as the flagship artist of Arista's new Nashville label, as well as his position as one of the most exciting members of the Class of '89.

The challenge would be to build upon his first brush with success and carve out a lasting place in Nashville—to be remembered not just as one of the best of his class, but as one of the most important artists of his time. To achieve such a goal, he would call upon the life skills instilled by his parents, and the first three decades of his life.

TWO

Southern Born

There's just something different about
growing up down in those parts. . . .
—ALAN JACKSON

Alan Eugene Jackson was born October 17,
1958, in Newnan, Georgia, about a half hour
southwest of Atlanta and just east of the
Chattahoochee River. The fifth child of Eugene
and Ruth Jackson, Alan has four older sisters:
Diane, twins Cathy and Carol, and Connie. "I
enjoyed being last," Alan said during a *Wichita
Eagle* interview in 1990. "I had the opportunity
to learn from their mistakes." Being the baby boy
in a house full of females, Alan received all the
attention he could handle—"I was always tag-
ging along," he noted in a *Wisconsin State Journal*
article.

And he is the first to admit that he was treated
as well as could be, keeping in mind the Jacksons
"never did have a lot of things." He credits the
women in the house for helping impart a strong

sense of empathy and respect for the opposite sex. "Maybe I'm a little more sensitive to certain things than some men are," he once told *Country America*.

> I probably got spoiled a little bit. All the girls looked after me.
> —ALAN JACKSON

Around the Jackson house, Alan was the little prince, but the family didn't live like royalty. According to Alan, his mom and dad set up housekeeping in a "toolshed" that was the core of the Jackson residence. Alan's grandparents had divided their farm and split the land among their children. Eugene and Ruth took their few acres, started a family, and added on to their home as they added kids to the fold.

Owing to the way the land was divided, Alan was able to reap the benefits of having his relatives as neighbors. His grandmother lived next door, and his cousins were on the adjacent plots. He had plenty of kids to play with and all their parents to watch over him. "We were like the Waltons, kind of," Alan has said. It gave him the deep sense of family and nostalgia that is still an integral part of his character.

"We weren't very well off financially. I mean, I had shoes, but I slept in the hall until I was ten years old, when my oldest sister went away to college." He remembers how cold it got on winter nights and recalls that his mother "would heat towels and wrap them around my feet before I went to bed." (And he still prefers to sleep in a cold bedroom.) At playtime, Alan fashioned makeshift toy cars by cutting pictures out of old magazines and attaching them to pasteboard. Yet it never would have occurred to him that his family was poor; his friends weren't better off, and the Jackson children never did without the necessities. At one point he had an exotic pet, a spider monkey named Peanuts.

Although three of Alan's sisters grew up to be schoolteachers (and the fourth married one), school wasn't his favorite spot on Earth. He did, however, do enough to keep up with his peers, and his teachers found him bright and creative. English was his strongest subject, as he had a knack for storytelling. "[The teacher would] give you one line and you had to create a story about it, and I was always good at that," Alan recalled in a 1990 interview. On the other hand, he was no budding Melville. "I don't read much or have all

13

that much of a vocabulary," he confesses.

Alan tended to procrastinate, a trait he carried through high school and into adulthood. "I've always been that way," he once explained in *Country Weekly.* "Even when I was back in school, I wouldn't do my book reports until the morning of the class." Not much has changed in that respect. Asked not long ago about what motivates him to write songs, Alan responded, "Usually, I've got to come up with songs for the next album. That's what triggers it!"

Most of the Nashville glitterati offer tales of their childhood musical exploits. Not Alan. "It seems that everyone wants to come up with a great story about music in their background, but it's not like I grew up with a guitar in my hands," he told David Meador in the *Roanoke Times.* In fourth grade, he gave his first public musical performance, lip-synching the Sam the Sham and the Pharoahs song "Li'l Red Riding Hood."

Aside from the odd church gathering or holiday sing-along, music wasn't a huge part of Alan's childhood. His mother sometimes sang to her son, which Alan remembers well. "She didn't have the greatest voice, but she always sang those old songs like 'Would You Like to Swing on a Star.'" Although his big sisters exposed him to some rock-and-roll and R&B, Alan observes, "We didn't buy records, and my parents didn't have a big stereo."

What singing he did as a youngster was limited to gospel and humming along with the wooden-box radio his father won in a contest. *Hee Haw*, a national television show devoted to country music, hit the airwaves when Alan was about eleven. "That was probably the earliest I remember being affected by real country music," Alan said in a 1999 press release. But as he also once remembered, in the *Knoxville News-Sentinel*, "I was a teenager before I got into George and Merle."

> Sometimes I feel like I grew up in a time warp . . . thirty years behind other people.
> —ALAN JACKSON

While his parents didn't steer him toward a singing career, they did stress the importance of working hard to reach his goals. "I don't know what they did, but my mom and dad raised us kids so that we'd all be successful at whatever we did," Alan has stated. At the age of twelve, Alan took his first job, working part-time in a shoe store. He saved his pennies until, in a few years, he'd earned enough—three thousand dollars—to buy a white 1955 Ford Thunderbird.

The car was a fixer-upper, but that was half the fun. "Daddy and I took it apart in the garage and restored it," Alan later told the *Greensboro News & Record*. "I wouldn't drive it in the rain." Alan's dad was a mechanic in a Ford factory, and he helped Alan bring the T-bird up to snuff. "That car was all I cared about," Alan told *People*. "It was like a member of the family."

Alan's dad passed a lifelong love of all things mechanical to his son, but he passed on a lot more: Call it a moral compass, or a blueprint for how a man should handle himself. Alan has said, "My father might be the only truly good man I've ever known. He's as honest as they come. If I turn out half as good, I'll be happy."

Eugene and Ruth also instilled in their children a desire to please others. "All my sisters are [that] way," he confessed in a 1991 interview. "No matter what we do, it's real important for people to like us."

Hard work and machines were the main themes of Alan's life from the time he could pick up a wrench. He was an average student, athletic but not a jock, and he did the typical things small-town teenagers do. Music wasn't a large part of Alan's out-of-school activities, but he did begin getting familiar with the guitar.

Legend has it that at one point Alan put in an application for a loan. The banker didn't come through with the cash, but he did end up giving Alan a few guitar lessons, and the two men later joined forces in a band. Those initial lessons from an experienced musician were crucial in Alan's development as a guitarist, but in general he doesn't place much stock in the value of formal musical instruction. Alan once told reporter Ina Pasch, "Training takes the soul out of your music and messes you up."

Not long before Alan took his first guitar lesson, his parents had purchased a stereo for the first time. Now he could listen to records at home and practice singing after school with a female friend with whom he formed an informal duo. The idea of being a musician took root in Alan's mind, even if he didn't give it serious consideration. A full four years passed before the idea started to bloom in full. Looking back, he recalls, "Music's the only thing I kept coming back to, but I didn't think at first that was any big deal." He told *TV Guide* in 1994, "It was more of a hobby in the beginning."

> I was far more interested in cars and girls
> for the whole rest of my early life than I was
> in writing songs.
> —ALAN JACKSON

Around this time, Alan "discovered" the father
of contemporary country, Hank Williams Sr. "I
kind of got wrapped up in him," Alan remembers
with deep fondness. It would be a surprise if a
teen in Alan's position wasn't compelled by the
saga of the former Hiram King Williams: superstar at twenty-five, corpse at twenty-nine, legend
for all time. Alan didn't want to follow in his
hero's self-destructive footsteps, but he looked to
ol' Hank's sound and style as a template. Years
later Alan cowrote a haunting tribute, "Midnight
in Montgomery," in honor of the tragic artist. He
told the *Phoenix Gazette*, "Hank is just the king of
country. I wanted to write a tribute to him."

Another seminal event was the opening of a
concert park in Newnan. When he was twenty
years old, Alan went to his first live music show
there. Headlining that night was the father-
daughter duo the Kendalls, who had won a 1977
CMA Award for Single of the Year with "Heaven's
Just a Sin Away." Years later he told the *San*

Antonio Express-News, "There was something about all those people clapping and cheering that fired me up." Taking in the onstage action and the offstage excitement, Alan thought to himself, I can do this! He was right, but it was nearly a decade before he got the chance.

> If I wasn't singing, I'd be in the automobile business, wheelin' and dealin'.
> —ALAN JACKSON

In the meantime, Alan was all about hard work and machines. For fun and to raise cash he repaired old cars, then sold them at a profit. In a 1990 interview he proclaimed, "You might think this is crazy, but this is the truth. I have owned and sold at least three hundred boats, cars, and motorcycles since the age of fifteen." On the other hand, in a 1994 interview he referred to himself as a "crummy" mechanic and not an outgoing salesman. Still, he must've done well enough to stick with it for as long as he did, and besides, it was a terrific way for a young person to get practical experience and earn spending money. He was no slacker; since that first job at age twelve, he did what he had to do to keep change in his pockets.

Long before stardom knocked, Alan drew a paycheck for selling shoes, janitorial supplies, and cars. He delivered furniture, helped build houses, rebuilt engines, and waited tables. He operated a forklift at Kmart, a job he described to Fred Shuster of the *Los Angeles Daily News*: "It was like being in prison every day. I hated punching that clock."

His parents were hard workers, too, of course. Alan's mother was a lunchroom worker in a bra factory, and his dad worked the same factory job for twenty-five years. Alan once told Brooks Whitney in the *Chicago Tribune*, "My parents taught me if you want something, you can do it. . . . You just have to be willing to work hard and put all your energy into it." When he sings about the life and times of the working person, you can be sure Alan knows what he's singing about.

Alan suggests that aspiring musicians—especially those who are striving to be country songwriters—should get out in the world and live a life separate from their art. He points out that in his case, there was a lot of living to do: different jobs, an unfinished attempt at college, and marriage at a young age. "I think a lot of people who are gung-ho about music from the beginning don't get a chance to really get out there and live," Alan explains. "And it's hard to write about life if you haven't lived."

THREE

Livin' on Love

He had the T-bird,
that was his biggest selling point.
—DENISE JACKSON

I married Denise
when she was too young to know better.
—ALAN JACKSON

You never know when the love of your life is going to pop up and say hello. Denise Jackson found that out when she was sixteen. She was sitting in the Dairy Queen after church on a Sunday evening in 1976. The spot was a designated hangout for local teens, and Denise had noticed a blond, lanky young man laughing and talking with his friends. Alan had a certain something that, years later, would spur a writer to call him "a 1990s version of Gary Cooper," handsome and easygoing. Denise didn't know that she and he shared the same last name, much less that they'd end up sharing their lives.

Alan noticed the pretty girl noticing him, the

23

way these things usually go, and he struck up a casual conversation. Sitting next to her, making chitchat, he dropped a penny down her blouse and joked about going in after it. Denise laughed and the small talk continued, but soon it was time for her to be heading home. Not long after Alan and Denise parted, Denise got into her mother's car and headed home. She'd driven just a couple of blocks when Alan popped up from the backseat, where he'd been hiding on the floorboard. A startled Denise just about leaped out of her skin, but she soon caught her breath and managed to see humor in the flirtatious trick. She cruised around for a while, then dropped Alan off without calling the police or punching his lights out.

The future couple had been introduced, but the romance didn't get started until later. Denise recounted in a 1994 *People* article, "I think what attracted him to me was that I didn't go out with him the first time he asked me. But he called three or four months later, and I felt differently." Denise and Alan were restless and young. The relationship ran a winding, organic course, sometimes off, sometimes on. Denise remembers, "We were just typical high school kids. We'd get mad at each other and break up. He'd go date somebody else to make me mad; I'd date the quarterback to make him mad. But we ended up back together."

As time passed, Alan and Denise were interwoven in the fabric of each other's lives. She finished high school and tried to figure out where to go from there; he took classes at West Georgia Community College and worked fixing and selling cars. On Christmas Eve 1978, Alan unveiled a huge surprise. "I was sitting on my mother's living room floor and he was getting that little box out and it scared me to death," Denise explained in the book *Nashville Wives*. "I thought, 'Surely this is going to be earrings.'"

Alan's proposal caught Denise off guard; after all, she was only eighteen, and they had never even broached the subject of marriage. It was a romantic and inspired act on Alan's part; a little bit out of character, too, considering this was the same man who once bought Denise a new car fender for Valentine's Day. Once she got past the shock, Denise answered yes, and although her finger now sports a ten-carat diamond masterpiece, she still treasures the half-carat ring Alan offered her that evening.

Alan and Denise were united December 15, 1979, with two hundred guests in attendance. Alan sang a nontraditional version of "The Wedding Song," and Denise reports that Alan was more nervous about his singing than about tying the knot. It was a perfect day for the newlyweds, and the first day of a marriage that would last through the best of times . . . and the hardest.

> He loves watching the sunset—he notices things like that. He's kind of romantic.
> —DENISE JACKSON

As soon as the wedding whirlwind had wound down, Alan and Denise set about finding a house they could call their own. Finding a first home was a project in itself, but it was made all the more difficult by the fact that Alan had to sell his car to raise the cash for a down payment. It would've been an almost unthinkable step not long before.

But his priorities had changed, and his new life with Denise was tops on the list. Years later, she carried the gesture full circle, tracking down the T-bird in North Carolina and bringing it back to Alan as a Christmas gift. At first he thought it was just a car that looked like the one he used to love, but when he said, "That looks like *my* car," Denise clued him in: "Alan, that *is* your car."

Alan just sat there in the driver's seat, over-whelmed. "He lost it," Denise recalls. "He cried. He couldn't even get out of the car for a minute." Alan jokes that while he gives his wife all sorts of shiny new gifts, she got him nothing but an old car. But obviously he treasures that old Thunderbird more than any other car in his collection. "So my life is really like a fairy tale," he proclaims. "I got my car back. What else can I have?"

Alan and Denise settled into married life, doing their best to make ends meet. The days of cruising the Dairy Queen and hanging out at Hilly's Mill on the river were fading. She taught school, he put his back into the blue-collar work that sometimes seemed would be his lot in life. It wasn't wine and roses, but the lovebirds were resilient, and their bond was strong. Denise and Alan discussed their plans for the future, which included children, a higher-salaried job for her, and perhaps a singing career for him. Alan was part of the local music scene, performing with a group called Dixie Steel.

In 1981, the year he turned twenty-three, Alan was influenced by the career turns of two people, one in Nashville and the other closer to home. First, at a time when the Urban Cowboy trend was in full force on country radio, George Strait's debut hit, "Unwound," was a revelation. The song not only launched Strait's career, it touched off the New Traditionalist movement that inspired the generation of New Country artists that followed. Alan was no exception. After he became a star and was cited as an influence on the next generation of artists, Alan commented, "I think that's the way I was when I came to town in '85 and George Strait was *the* artist."

While the great Mr. Strait had a massive formative influence on Alan's musical pursuits, the accomplishments of a person who wasn't in the public eye motivated Alan almost as much. Word came down the Newnan grapevine that a former classmate of Alan's, who often spoke of becoming an airline pilot, had attained his goal and started flying for American Airlines. The news was an inspiration to Alan, who saw that a local boy could achieve his aspirations on a national scale. "It made me realize a dream can come true if you don't mind working for it," Alan later declared.

In a small town, you have to understand, you go to school, then you go to college, then you get married and you have a kid or two. Something like singing in Nashville or having a record out, that was just another world.

—ALAN JACKSON

Still, it wasn't until 1985 that he decided to reach for the brass ring. Denise had taken a job with Piedmont Airlines as a flight attendant and would be training in Greensboro for about six months. "It was the first time we'd ever been apart," Alan later recalled in the *Detroit Free Press*. He was on his own, with nothing to do but work and go home—and his focus turned to music. There was a dock near their trailer, and Alan would sit out there and try to come up with song ideas. Years later he described the period by saying, "I didn't really have anything to do except fish, work at the marina, and write songs." Alan isn't eager to remember the bulk of those initial stabs at composition, which, in his words, were "pretty bad."

His songwriting efforts were motivated in part

by a friend's suggestion that Alan couldn't make it big in Nashville singing other people's songs. "I didn't know anything about it," Alan later revealed. "Somebody said, 'If you go to Nashville, you need your own songs. You can't go up there singing everybody else's things.' So I decided I'd try to write something." In another interview, he put it simply, "There wasn't a lot of song-pitching going on in Newnan."

It was the catalyst for Alan to get started, spurring him to create some of his best material: songs such as "I'd Love You All Over Again," which was written on a rainy morning during a five-night stint at Bad Bob's in Pine Bluff, Arkansas. It was to become Alan's first *Billboard* No. 1. "I wrote that song last summer," he told a San Antonio radio programmer in late December 1990, "because our tenth wedding anniversary was coming up. I never thought it would make the album, let alone be a single. It's pretty wild that it was shipped out on our anniversary."

Denise was more than an inspiration for Alan. She would later recount in *In Style*, "We worried we'd get divorced when I started with Piedmont because I'd be away so much. But it ended up being the ultimate job." One night in the Atlanta airport she was waiting for a flight, when who should she notice sitting in a lounge area but

Glen Campbell, the Nashville legend who recorded such mammoth hits as "Witchita Lineman," "Galveston," "Southern Nights," and "Rhinestone Cowboy."

> ". . . Excuse me, my husband's about to move to Nashville to be a singer-songwriter. What does he need to do? . . ."
> —DENISE JACKSON

Denise had the gumption to approach Campbell and ask if he had some advice for her husband, who, she explained, was considering moving to Nashville to pursue a dream. "When I saw Glen," Denise recalled in a 1996 interview on the Nashville Network's *Soulmates*, "I said to myself, 'This is the chance, go for it.' I don't usually approach people at the airport, so it was hard to do, but I did it." It turned out to be a stroke of genius, but you might not have known it at first. Alan notes, "That was a weird chance meeting that my wife ran into him. It took several years for all of that to really help me."

There's an old adage that refers to the fact that to make it in Music City, with very few exceptions, you must live and work there—"You must be present to win." Campbell confirmed what the Jacksons suspected: The move to Music City was a must. But he went a step further, offering Denise his business card and an invitation for Alan to drop in to the offices of Campbell's publishing company.

Denise couldn't wait to tell her husband about the encounter, and he was pumped when he heard the news. That cinched it. Alan was determined to chase the neon rainbow up to Tennessee. But first there were negotiations to settle in the Jackson household. "I was happy living in Georgia," Denise asserts, "so Alan and I made a deal. We would move to Nashville, but if he didn't land a record deal within five years we would move back to Georgia." Roughly one month later, in mid-August 1985, Alan paid his first visit to the capital of country music.

FOUR

Dreamin' It Real

I had no earthly idea what a publisher was,
or a producer, or anything. I just wanted
to carry on the tradition of real country music.
—ALAN JACKSON

Hat in hand, Alan headed for the offices of Glen Campbell Music. The manager Alan met, Marty Gamblin, recalled in a *Country Weekly* article, "He was wearing jeans, tennis shoes, and a baseball cap—and it was all 'Yes, sir' and 'No, sir.' " Mr. Gamblin sang the familiar refrain: "If you're serious, you need to get you a job and move up here." A couple of weeks later, Alan did just that. He recalls of that first meeting at Campbell's office, "When I got to town, I went to see them right away, and played them a tape of songs I'd written. They thought I was a better singer than songwriter and couldn't give me a job."

"Things were going slow at first. The money wasn't exactly rolling in," he later told the *Dallas Morning News*. But soon he landed a job in the mailroom at The Nashville Network. There is something poetic about a future TNN superstar sorting mail in the basement in his pre-fame days, but it almost didn't happen. The first place Alan checked out as a potential place of employment was a shop that fashioned fiberglass boats. He later told the *Greensboro News & Record,* "It was 110 degrees and fumes about to kill me, so I decided I didn't want to do that."

This is one of the most misunderstood chapters in Alan's life. He has tried to set the record straight, explaining, "Some people think I took the job to study up on the music business and learn the ropes. The way I've heard it told, it sounds like I stepped from the mailroom to the chair next to Ralph Emery just like that. The truth is, though, that I took the job because I needed the money."

The Nashville Network mailroom wasn't exactly the nerve center of the Nashville music scene, but it had benefits. "A lot of people that worked there were also people that had been in the music business one time or another, so I'd go around and ask questions," Alan explained. "It was a lot better place for me to be at the time than some garage down the street." He wasn't making much money, but thankfully Denise was doing well at the airline.

Dreamin' It Real

> I did drag her away from her family and friends to come up here and live in a basement for five years while she paid the bills.
>
> —ALAN JACKSON

With their combined incomes, Alan and Denise were able to afford a small basement apartment. Denise asserts that she loved the little place, despite the shortage of space and natural light. Nancy Jones, the wife of George Jones, said in her book *Nashville Wives* that after the Jacksons had their first child, Mattie, they brought her to the Joneses' house, and she fussed the entire time. Alan suggested, "You'd cry too if you were seeing windows for the first time."

Of course, it was just Alan and Denise in the apartment until Mattie's birth in 1990. Their hands were full enough, with Denise traveling for the airline and Alan trying to spark his music career. "We always seemed to make ends meet, we just never had a lot left over for any luxuries," remembers Alan. He tried to focus on his song-writing and chase down a record deal, while Denise carried much of the financial load.

When the couple wasn't overworking, at times

they'd set out in an old boat on Hickory Lake to do some "stargazing." Alan once told *Country* magazine, complete with an affected drawl, "And we'd sit out there in front of Barbara Mandrell's house: ' . . . Ah think that's her. Ah see somebody walkin' in the house.' "

Years later, it would be Alan's turn to deal with gawkers—at the Center Hill Lake house he dubbed the Real World. Asked if he ever got tired of fans coming to his dock and hollering for a glimpse, he had to confess, "Yeah, sometimes, like when your hair's greasy and your stomach's hangin' over your swimsuit and they're shootin' a video of you."

In 1986 Alan got a big break, as the Glen Campbell connection at last paid off with more than advice and encouragement. Alan's music skills had sharpened to the point that he was granted a hundred-dollar-per-month stipend as an in-house songwriter. A more ideal job would've been hard to imagine. Unlike the mailroom at TNN, this was a position on the pulse of the music business. Many people feel that landing a job as a staff writer is a big step to gaining credibility in Nashville.

> There's no need for everybody to breathe
> cigarette smoke every night in the clubs if
> they don't have to. But in my case, it was
> good for me. I learned a lot about people
> and about music. And I got good song
> ideas out of those years of paying my dues.
> —ALAN JACKSON

The songwriting gig also freed Alan to assemble a touring band, as he didn't need to keep strict office hours. In the coming months, Alan would see the inside of "every dive from Miami to Missouri and Texas to the East Coast." With his sidekicks, the Strayhorns, Alan toured the honky-tonks, dance halls, and dive bars of West Virginia, Ohio, and Pennsylvania.

Former manager Barry Coburn says, "Alan would play four sets a night on Friday and Saturday at some club in West Virginia, then drive all the way back to Nashville the next day." Alan and his Strayhorns even strayed as far as Maryland and Canada in search of fans. "We had a van, a trailer, and I had a lady booking me," he remembers.

Alan also performed in southern states like Alabama, Louisiana, and, of course, Texas. It wasn't a glamorous life: drunken crowds in smoke-filled juke joints, late nights in cheap motels, and the occasional unreasonable club owner. Alan once explained, "It could be said that you needed [a handgun], just to make sure you got paid your money at the end of the night."

In those days, Alan was forced to perform mostly covers, and most of those had to be of current hits, including rock-and-roll. "Of course, I didn't do much of that," Alan told *Boston Globe* reporter Steve Morse in 1994, "but usually a couple of guys in my band would sing a couple of rock songs that would make [the bar owners] happy." Alan never failed to slip in a few of the classics from Merle Haggard, George Jones, or Gene Watson, and he served up some of his own material as well. A few lucky folks out there got to hear songs like "Here in the Real World," "Chasin' That Neon Rainbow," and "Someday," long before any of those songs were No. 1 hits.

For four years, Alan pounded the Music Row pavement in search of a record deal. "I got passed on for years. I told everybody I was too country for Nashville," Alan told reporter Diane Samms Rush. A few execs who listened to his demo passed along words of encouragement; at least one told him point-blank that he'd never be a star. "Some of those things really hurt," Alan later confided to

Jack Hurst of the *Chicago Tribune*. "Most of the time, though, what it did was make me more determined to prove them wrong. It made me madder."

One who did recognize Alan's potential was Barry Coburn. A native New Zealander, he had been a concert promoter in Australia and was a devout fan of country music. Barry and his wife, Jewel, had moved to Nashville to make their living in music publishing and managing. The first tape Alan brought to Barry contained only covers of other people's songs, but Barry told Alan to bring in the cassettes of his own material. "Nobody really likes my songs; they're not very good," Alan reportedly told Barry, who recalls, "The first song on the tape was, I think, 'Wanted.' That's all I needed to hear to know that Alan had it."

"Wanted" would become the second Top 5 single of Alan's career. In a press release he noted that he wrote it while sitting on the couch alone one night strumming his guitar and half watching an old John Wayne western he'd seen numerous times. "As John walked into a sheriff's office," explained Alan, "I looked up above his head and saw a wanted poster." Alan penned the first verse and chorus right there, then put the song away for six months and, one afternoon while working with songwriter Charlie Craig, "pulled out 'Wanted' and finished it."

Alan's troubles, of course, were prior to the boom in country music that Alan and the Class of '89 set off. Otherwise, an artist of his talent would've been snapped up by a major label in three shakes of a lamb's tail. As it was, things moved at a snail's pace, and Alan often lamented to Barry and Jewel that, although he was pushing thirty, he still didn't have a recording contract. Barry told reporter Michael Corcoran, "He'd come to the office and the first thing out of his mouth was always, 'Well, did you get me a record deal?'"

"I was being turned down by every label in town, twice," Alan remembers. "It didn't look very promising for a few years there." Barry pushed Alan to keep working on his songs and his stage presence. While he had faith in Alan's talent, Barry knew that it would be easier if Alan were connected with other talented people. "He hooked me up with a lot of good writers and helped me get a tape together," Alan has said of Barry.

I like collaborating, because if I didn't, I'd probably never finish a song.
—ALAN JACKSON

One of the writers was Mark Irwin, who copenned "Here in the Real World." Alan notes, "We're as different as night and day. I'm from Georgia and Mark is from New Jersey. But we got together and kicked around a few ideas. I played Mark those two lines and he loved them. In less than an hour, the song that started my career was written." Another was Zack Turner, who says of Alan, "He's real, real headstrong about keeping his stuff country, true to his roots."

For what became Alan's third Top 5 single, "Chasin' That Neon Rainbow," he enlisted the help of a top Nashville songsmith. "Jim McBride and I were writing together for the first time," Alan once explained in a press release, "and we were talking about my life in Georgia and the experience of playing in the honky-tonk circuit. I remembered a radio that my daddy won when I was a young child and how my mama used to sing to my sisters and me. I also remembered how my mama hated for me to play in the bars. All those things set the story in motion, and within a few sessions my life chasing that neon rainbow was set to music."

Jim and Alan had a mutual positive effect on each other's career. Jim had come to Music City in 1982 after Conway Twitty recorded one of his songs. But his career didn't take off until he hooked up with Alan. "Definitely the turning was meeting Alan Jackson," Jim told *Knoxville News-Sentinel* writer Wayne Bledsoe. "The first time we sat down together he played me 'Home' and I played him 'Dixie Boy.' Both songs were sort of the stories of our lives."

Jim and Alan also cowrote "Someday," the second single from *Don't Rock the Jukebox* and Alan's third straight *Billboard* No. 1. It was Jim's idea to write a song about the fact that just about everybody has said at some point in their life: I'm going to do this someday. Alan has noted, "Sometimes someday never comes." He also explained, "That's what this song is about in relation to a couple in love." In 1991 and 1992, "Chasin' That Neon Rainbow" and "Someday" won kudos at the Music City News Songwriters Awards.

Another important collaborator Alan met during this period was Wichita Falls, Texas native Keith Stegall. Although just a bit older than Alan, Keith was a veteran of the business when the two men were introduced in 1988. In fact, Keith had started on piano at age four, and he first performed at age eight. Over the course of his career, he had delved into rock, rhythm and blues, country, folk, gospel, and lounge music. Keith moved to Nashville and had a handful of Top 40 hits in the mid-1980s, then turned to writing songs for other artists.

Alan considered Keith one of the best singer-songwriters around, and he was eager for Keith to produce him. "I kept beating him up to record me until finally one day he agreed to do it," Alan recalled. There was no disappointment from either side. Working with Alan has been the crown jewel in Keith's career as a producer, which includes credits with Terri Clark, Sammy Kershaw, and Billy Ray Cyrus. "He lets me be myself," Alan cites as the main reason he loves working with Keith. "I had worked with a couple of guys who wanted to take me in a different direction . . . and it never worked."

There was one drawback to this period of making and mailing demo tapes that Alan couldn't anticipate. According to a small article in the *Memphis Commercial-Appeal,* in October 1991 Alan was forced to file suit to stop the release of eleven recordings he'd made in the mid-1980s. Much, if not all, of the work was of demonstration quality, not intended for release to the public. It was the type of problem that often confronts a famous artist who once had to do whatever it took to make ends meet.

But, for the most part, Alan can look back on this time as a catalyst of career growth. His demos started to attract serious attention from major labels. Alan played three showcase gigs, and a handful of A&R reps expressed interest in him. Barry also made sure that Alan's demo was being heard by all the important ears on Music Row. One such pair belonged to Tim DuBois, head of the new Arista-Nashville label.

Tim had lived in Music City since 1977. Back then, he earned his keep as a songwriter, and in the early 1980s he penned three No. 1 hits. Tim turned to managing in 1985, putting together an Eagles-esque ensemble known as Restless Heart. Tim's country-rock songwriting and the band's perfect harmonizing produced a string of six straight chart-toppers. He stopped managing in 1988 and took on the exciting task of building a new label from the ground up.

One of the first demos Tim received was from Barry Coburn. Impressed, he called Barry to find out when he could catch the artist's act in person. Barry told Tim that Alan would be onstage at Douglas Corner the following week. It wasn't convenient for Tim, who planned to be in Los Angeles on the evening Alan was scheduled to perform. Barry explained that his client might not be doing another showcase, as he already had a couple of major labels sniffing around.

Tim didn't want to take the risk that Alan might

sign with someone else, so he altered his plans and was in the audience at the Douglas Corner Café on the night of Alan's gig. It was a wise choice. The bar had been the site of many showcases, but this one proved to be special: the night that launched Alan Jackson. Tim was in search of a flagship artist for Arista-Nashville, and he found what he wanted that evening.

> I saw in him a unique writing talent, coupled with an identifiable voice. . . . He hadn't been in Nashville so long that he had been polluted by the way we Nashville tunesmiths write things.
>
> —TIM DUBOIS

Alan didn't bring the house down but did deliver a workmanlike nine-song performance. His style, his sound, and his good looks were in evidence, and that was what had Tim agog. At the end of the show, he approached Barry and told him flat-out, "I want him." The hard struggle for recognition was about to get easier. "Back during the first three years I lived in Nashville, I never thought I'd make it," Alan remembered.

The next morning a meeting was set up

between Barry, Alan, Tim, and Tim's boss, Clive Davis. Alan almost didn't make it; he'd banged his head fixing a boat trailer. "It's bleeding," he told Barry, "can't do it." But minutes before the meeting, Alan arrived, dressed in his trademark western boots, hat, and jacket. Clive laid out a list of reasons that Alan should sign with Arista, mostly having to do with Clive's resumé, which includes work with the Allman Brothers, Bruce Springsteen, and the Grateful Dead. "It was an incredible pitch," Barry has said.

Alan had said next to nothing during the meeting, but before leaving he told Clive, "I'm glad I didn't know about you, because if I had I sure would've been too scared to come." It was classic Alan, a blend of aw-shucks naïveté and cutting insight. Clive's impressive pitch notwithstanding, Barry wanted to mull over the offer before signing, much to the chagrin of every other person in the room. Alan left the office without a contract, but the next day Barry got Tim on the phone and accepted the deal.

> The first thing I did after getting my recording contract was buy Denise a push-button phone. She'd always wanted one but I could never afford it.
> —ALAN JACKSON

Alan offered, "Tim said they were looking for somebody just like me. He said the whole Nashville industry would probably think they were going to try to drag pop music into country, and they wanted somebody like me as a statement that they were here to make country music." While some might have questioned the credentials of the new label—Arista was firmly established in the pop realm but a no-name in Nashville—the Jackson camp was pleased as punch with the situation. "They were new to country music," Alan later reflected, "but they had a good track record for having a lot of faith and confidence in their artists."

No one grasped better than Alan that this was the break he had been working to earn. "I had watched a lot of artists come and go," he explained, "so I knew when I got my record deal that it was a huge step for me." Alan also confessed to being aware that "I may have one or two hits and then disappear. Or I may not hit at all."

FIVE

Catchin' That Rainbow

> I hoped my career would be just huge,
> of course, but I was also very realistic
> about what happens in this business.
> —ALAN JACKSON

Just as Alan had been "spoiled" as a kid, being
the only boy in a house full of females, he enjoyed
the benefits of being the lone artist in Arista-
Nashville's lineup. Sure, in the years that followed,
the label would be home to Brooks & Dunn, Pam
Tillis, Steve Wariner, Diamond Rio, BR5-49, and
others. But in 1988 it was all about Alan Jackson.
Tim needed to hit one out of the park with his
first swing, and he put all his time and energy into
Alan's career.

So did Barry, who set his mind to refining
Alan's onstage efforts. The handsome singer
looked and sounded great, but he wasn't Garth
Brooks. Jumping around and whooping it up just
wasn't Alan's style. As it turned out, he didn't need
to do those things to please his fans. Alan stirred a

different kind of exhilaration by being his laid-back self, telling stories about his father and his childhood, and flashing that Alan smile.

The stage wasn't Alan's natural habitat; in fact, he came across as downright awkward at times. As late as May 1991 he admitted, "I'm real uncomfortable onstage. . . . My wife says I'm crazy. . . . She says the reason I like performing is that it's one way I can be in a crowd and still be separated from 'em." In some respects Alan's shyness was charming because it emphasized his regular-guyness.

He recalls his first time playing in San Antonio, asking a reporter, "Do you think any people will show up?" Actually, not many did, but Alan didn't get too uptight about it. Standing at the edge of the Blue Bonnet Palace stage, he was chatting it up with anyone who felt like talking. Apparently there weren't many takers, as one reporter observed, and Alan was later heard to say, "I'd always heard people were friendly in Texas. Guess I've caught them on a bad night."

But there's another side to the coin: Most folks want their stars to seem bigger than life. It's been said that the stage is God's left hand, and Alan once noted, "When I used to go see people sing, it almost—I hate to say it—put 'em up on a pedestal for me. It was like they had some kind of power, like a preacher or something." It was part of Alan's job to tap into the innate stage presence buried beneath his shyness.

Barry analyzed Alan's stage routine—his patter and movements—and helped him seem more at ease in the spotlight. It paid off big time when Alan opened for Randy Travis on 1991's Heroes and Friends Tour. Barry anted up for Alan to use the huge video screens usually reserved for the head-liner, and the effect was dramatic: There was an unexpected power in his no-nonsense approach, a power that shone through on the big screens. "Alan reminds me very much of Randy in the early days," said Lib Hatcher, Randy's wife and manager. "The voice and music are there, as is the shyness that audiences find so appealing."

While he understood the value of being well-perceived as a personality, Alan's primary focus was on the music. He was far from being a pol-ished performer, and every gig gave him a new opportunity to refine and develop his skills. "The more you sing the better you're supposed to get and the more you find your own voice," he asserted in a 1990 interview.

In the fall of 1989, Alan entered a Nashville recording studio with a pair of producers: Keith Stegall and Scott Hendricks. Scott had been a member of Restless Heart, the group Tim put together in the mid-1980s, and he handled a good chunk of the production duties for them. It was a coup for him to be included on the debut project of a major new label. Scott went on to produce Brooks & Dunn, then took a job as the head of Capitol-Nashville.

It took less than a week for Alan to lay down the basic tracks, and a month later the album—*Here in the Real World*—was ready for release. "When you combine [luck and timing] together with somebody who stands firmly on what they believe and the kind of music they want to do, it becomes clear what to do," Keith commented.

Nine of the ten tunes were written or cowritten by Alan, a very rare occurrence in Nashville, where the songwriting is often done by hired guns. Of course, Alan had been one of those hired guns while working for Glen Campbell, and he kept a cardboard box that contained the best songs he had written. It existed well before he got famous, and after Alan hit the big time, he'd sift through that collection each time he entered the studio to create a new album.

He is what he is. I try to stay out of the way as much as I can.
—KEITH STEGALL

The first single, "Blue Blooded Woman," wasn't a hit. According to Alan, "My single died a hard death and my wife was pregnant." But it did put radio programmers on notice that Alan Jackson was one worth watching. Alan's next single, "Here in the Real World," got a lot more support from radio. This was the song that had almost been a single for Tony Perez a couple of years earlier, the song Alan thought was a bit too "rangy" for him. It soared to No. 1 in *Radio & Records*, becoming the first of four megahits off *Here in the Real World*. The album went gold before the end of 1990, and it remained a solid seller after passing multiplatinum levels.

Alan was at Arista's anniversary concert in mid-March, mingling with the likes of Barry Manilow and Whitney Houston at Radio City Music Hall. "I was definitely the only one there in a cowboy hat," Alan joked. One of the best parts of the experience came back at the hotel, where Alan received flowers and best wishes from one of his musical idols: George Jones.

Critical consensus holds that "Possum" Jones is the greatest male vocalist in country music history, and his impact on Alan's music is clear. "He set the standard of what a country song is, and how it should be sung," Alan has said. Jones started as a honky-tonker, singing classics such as "White

Lightning" in the 1950s. In the 1960s he began to develop a reputation as Nashville's premier balladeer, scoring huge hits with "Tender Years" and "She Thinks I Still Care." He opened the 1970s with "A Good Year for the Roses," and kicked off the 1980s with "He Stopped Loving Her Today."

"I've never even met him," Alan told a reporter, a bit stunned to be getting attention from his musical idol. Coming from one of the most famous artists in the business, George's support could mean a lot to a newcomer. It sure meant a lot to Alan, who voiced his desire to record with the legend. "I've got this song I've been saving for three years that everybody wanted me to pitch to Randy Travis for his duet album. But I wouldn't do it. I wanted to keep it and see if I ever got a shot to do it with George Jones." Alan not only got his wish, he and Denise were destined to become close friends with George and his wife, Nancy.

The rest of old-school Nashville took to Alan, too. He put in a couple of matinee stints at the Grand Ole Opry in spring and summer of 1990, then made his official debut in October. At that point, Alan had three hit singles under his belt: "Here in the Real World," "Wanted," and "Chasin' That Neon Rainbow." That same night Garth Brooks was inducted as a member, and there was talk that in Garth and Alan the future of Nashville might be present.

Throughout the first half of the decade, the press fixated on the idea that laid-back Alan and outgoing Garth were rivals, battling for the title King of Country. The two artists often went head-to-head in major award categories, with Garth dominating, starting with his taking of the CMA Horizon Award in 1990. Look at the CMA results for 1991 and 1992: six trophies for Mr. Brooks, including a clean sweep both years in the Entertainer and Album categories.

Despite being older than his counterpart, Alan's hit streak postdated Garth's by almost a year, and in general he seemed less driven to be the most popular performer on the planet. In other words, Garth was younger, more focused, and had gotten off to a head start. That said, Alan had surpassed Clint Black as Garth's top challenger. That Alan was perceived as more humble and traditional than Garth in part explains why the press often seemed to favor Alan. For instance, a staff writer for one Virginia metro daily wrote in 1992: "Forget Garthmania. The smart money is on Alan Jackson to outlast the current wave of country-music hysteria and endure as a Nashville artist who might still be around ten years from now."

> I don't sense any rivalry between me and
> Garth. But they always seem to bring up his
> name in reference to mine.
> —ALAN JACKSON

Of course, the "rivalry" was never really an
issue except in the press, but Alan did from time
to time poke a little fun at the rock-and-roll
antics that made Garth's concerts the talk of the
town. "I could go out there and run back and
forth or drive a tractor onstage; you do anything
like that and the crowd's going to get excited and
scream. But to me it takes away from the music.
To me, it's a lot harder to stand up there and sing
your song and entertain the crowd," Alan once
explained at a video conference of the Television
Critics Association.

Alan told a newspaper reporter in North
Carolina, "There are a lot of acts, some who open
for me, who are having to do the kind of entertaining onstage that he does, and there's nothing
wrong with that." April 1994 brought a *TV Guide*
article on Garth that included a side piece on Alan
titled "Garth's Nightmare?" The writer didn't suggest that there was bad blood between Alan and
Garth; in fact, he stressed that Alan "doesn't spend

much time wondering if he'll bump Garth Brooks from his throne."

Still, the title of the article implied that Alan might be on the verge of stealing Garth's thunder, an idea that Alan found laughable. His friend Gary Overton, who also became Alan's manager in 1994, told Richard Cromelin of the *Los Angeles Times*, "Alan looked at the story and he looked at me and said, 'Boo. Do I scare you? I don't believe I scare Garth either.'"

> Ten years ago I was driving a forklift at the Kmart warehouse and nobody was screaming at me then. I guess it's the magic of show business."
> —ALAN JACKSON

Another topic the media hyped was the influx of hunks-in-hats. The rise of New Country was tied in part to the sex appeal of the artists, and Alan had his share to offer in that area. He was featured in an *Entertainment Tonight* spot on "country hunks." His take on the subject: "Oh, I guess it's kind of flattering. I've been called a lot worse."

It was a rare media report that didn't at least touch on the subject of Alan's "assets." He was one of *Playgirl*'s Ten Sexiest Men and *People*'s 50 Most Beautiful People in 1992. He was showered with stageside gifts at each concert. "This is the first time I've been on stage with a big chocolate chip cookie at my feet during the show," Alan announced at a concert in Buffalo.

> It helps if you have good looks. But I'm not saying that's what sells records. There has to be talent in there, too.
> —ALAN JACKSON

Alan found himself answering questions about his effect on female fans, a discomforting position for a married man not used to seeing himself as an object of desire. "He's welcomed to the stage with adoring shrieks and has been tackled by female fans," Sophia Dembling told *Dallas Morning News* readers. Alan was kind of embarrassed about the attention, and more so by the suggestions of Arista personnel that he look for excuses to flash his derriere on stage. "I try not to turn around and get a drink of water or anything," he explained to Jack Hurst of the *Chicago Tribune*.

The phenomenon first became apparent at Billy Bob's in Fort Worth, where Alan and his band opened for Ricky Van Shelton, who was hot as a pistol on the charts. It was a big gig for Alan, but he wasn't the main attraction; the club directed Alan and his band to a small stage in the middle of the club about two feet from the dance floor. "Me and the band walked out, and it was wall-to-wall people right up in our faces," Alan recounted in the *Chicago Tribune*, "screaming from the time we started till we stopped. . . . It shocked me and scared my band to death."

Denise trusted Alan; their bond was tried and solid. "We've been married a pretty long time, so she's pretty secure," asserted Alan in a newspaper interview. "In fact, my wife's kind of tickled that people find her ol' husband attractive." They were expecting their first child in June, an event that would be the pinnacle in a year of peaks. "I heard her say as long as they're buying the records and putting shoes on the baby, she won't mind."

Still, it couldn't have been easy for Denise. She was coping with the sudden death of her brother and with Alan spending more time on the road than at home. Not long ago, they'd had only each other, but now he was being pulled in different directions. With a handful of Top 5 hits and a basket of awards proclaiming him the hottest new face in the business, it was all he could do to keep his feet on the ground. "You don't have anything in the beginning," Alan explained to Kimmy Wix in *Music City News*. "Then all of a sudden you've got everything and everybody is telling you how great you are. That can really mess with your mind if you're not careful."

She walks a little bit and falls down a lot.
—ALAN on Mattie Denise at ten months

On June 19, 1990, Mattie Denise Jackson (named for her grandmother and mother) was born. The arrival of their first child was truly a blessed moment for Denise and Alan, but it was also stressful. The bills needed to be paid, and Denise's flight attendant career was grounded. Alan has said, "The first year or two was rough because our first daughter was born right about the time my career was just getting started. . . . I guess I didn't really get to appreciate Denise's pregnancy, the birth, and that whole first year. . . . I was just so busy and committed to my career."

Alan's time was under extreme demand, and Denise was under intense pressure. She had a six-month-old to care for and a husband who couldn't be there as much as he wanted to be. "Denise would come over to sit with my wife, Cherie, and kind of cry on her shoulder because of the loneliness of Alan being gone so much," remembers Marty Gamblin.

Thanks to the support of their friends and the strength of their love, Alan and Denise got through a period that could have wrecked a less committed relationship. Alan learned that God, indeed, works in mysterious ways. "He knew it was going to be so crazy for me this year that I needed something that was going to help me keep my feet on the ground," Alan told reporter Jack Hurst.

> You need to keep your perspective. You have to remember where you came from.
> —ALAN JACKSON

While things were a little tumultuous at home, life on the road was hectic, too, if not as stressed. "It's a lot of fun. It's wide open," Alan professed. The quality of Alan's gigs was up. He opened for the Judds on their River of Time tour, performed at Farm Aid IV, and shared a bill with Clint Black, opening for CMA Artists of the Decade Alabama. (A critic noted: "Jackson and Black both delivered tight sets of raw-edged honky-tonk and western swing that made Alabama look weak by comparison.") Alan was the opener for George Strait at the Iowa State Fair, and the experience caused an epiphany. "I sat back and watched his show," Alan recalls, "and listened to him sing his songs, and it hit me where I was and what I was doing."

Alan's acclaim was spreading fast, and in late winter he appeared on *Geraldo* with Clint Black, K. T. Oslin, and Lorrie Morgan—some of the brightest lights of New Country. "He really didn't get in there and hammer away at us about anything bad," Alan joked to *San Antonio Light* reporter Carl Becker. Slowly but surely, Alan Jackson's name was creeping into the public consciousness.

His name was certainly in the minds of the members of the Country Music Association. At the twenty-fourth CMA Awards, he was nominated for the Horizon Award, Single and Song of the Year ("Here in the Real World"), and Album of the Year. Alan admitted to reporter Mark Morrison, "It's something I dreamed about for years." But when the winners were announced, Alan was left out. "There's always that flicker of hope that you might win," Alan confessed.

Despite going 0-for-4, his performance of "Here in the Real World" and the numerous mentions of his name added to his growing fan base. It's amazing to think that the song almost wasn't included on Alan's debut album. "It was our last night, our last session," he revealed in the *San Antonio Light*. "We just crammed it in there." November found Alan getting back to the real world himself. "I took a few days off and it was nice to get off the road and spend time with my family," he told writer Wiley Alexander. "I guess that's what I miss the most."

SIX

Hold on Tight

I'm definitely doing better than I've ever done,
which isn't saying much.
—ALAN JACKSON

In a span of just fifteen months, Alan's life had turned 180 degrees. He had a skyrocketing career and unlimited prospects. The first part of February 1991 featured an appearance at the American Music Awards in Los Angeles. ("Well, shoot, I'd rather be in Newnan than out here," Alan teased.) Exciting as that was, it couldn't compare to the news that "I'd Love You All Over Again" had hit No. 1 in *Billboard.*

Alan had seen each of his earlier singles reach the top spot on various other charts, but this was his first on the list most people think of as the standard. Strange as it might seem, Alan had to be convinced to include the song on the album in the first place. "I thought it was real special and too personal, but everybody else thought it should be on the album," Alan told an

LIVIN' ON COUNTRY

Atlanta Journal-Constitution staff writer.

Big things were happening back home, too. Denise and Alan were able to move out of the basement apartment they'd called home for the past five years. The move was especially welcome, now that Mattie Denise was in the picture. The days of cramped quarters were behind them, and eventually the Jacksons would be settled into a house twenty miles outside of Nashville and building a sprawling vacation home nicknamed the Real World.

An honest-to-goodness dream come true for Alan and Denise, the Real World features a knotty pine floor, exposed ceiling beams, and a plethora of antiques, as well as a redwood deck with a hot tub built flush in—as Alan wryly told *Country* magazine, "Most hot tubs you put a cover on and you can't walk on 'em. This one you can." The overriding characteristic of the Real World is its location, smack on the shore of Center Hill Lake. Alan keeps a full armada of boats, from fast ones for water-skiing to bass boats to a cabin cruiser.

In fall 1994, with his fame established and his focus centering more and more on his wife and children, Alan would tell *In Style*, "I've reached a plateau where I never thought I'd be, and Denise and I can finally put down some roots." The rough architectural design for the Real World was conceived by Denise and Alan and drawn by Alan, then a professional builder and an architect joined forces to make the idea a reality.

Although their primary residence was a colonial-style farmhouse outside Nashville (and they have another place in Florida), Alan and Denise would escape to the lake house when the need arose to get free of the grind. Alan was all too aware of the unreal aspects of fame—"the showbiz and all"—and going to the woods with his family made perfect sense: It was a means of escaping back to the real world.

Of course most people's conception of the real world doesn't include the luxury of Denise and Alan's top-floor master bedroom, which *In Style* writer Martha Hume described as "an airy white fantasy," complete with a stone fireplace and arched floor-to-ceiling windows. The room opens onto a deck with a view of the lake and woods. Alan volunteered, "Sometimes I wake up and it's so beautiful I can't go back to sleep."

Alan's road digs were roomier, too. His new tour bus was a giant step up from the van and trailer that had served Alan and his band in the days before fame. Alan was fighting a slight case of flu—"I'm about to whup that thang," he told reporter Russ DeVault—and focusing on an opening slot on tour with New Traditionalist pioneer Randy Travis.

The Insider's Country Music Handbook reveals that when Alan started working in the mailroom at TNN, Randy was slopping slaw as a short-order cook across the street at the Nashville Palace. But in 1986, when Alan was still singing in nightclubs, hacking out a living, dreaming of the elusive record deal, Randy was retooling the genre with *Storms of Life*, one of the most impressive debut albums ever put out. (Keep in mind that in 1985 the *New York Times* ran an article declaring country music D.O.A., then one year later welcomed its return.)

That album served as a link between the back-to-basics aesthetic of George Strait and the muscular production techniques that define New Country. Alan confirmed Randy's influence on him in a 1991 interview, "Even after Randy hit as big as he did, record labels would tend to sign acts slicker or smoother. I was a young man who loved hard-core country music, and I figured there were other people out there who did, too."

Five years later, Randy was feeling the heat from a wave of new singers, one of whom was Alan. The double bill of Jackson and Travis had all the drawing power promoters could ask. Ron Wynn, a concert reviewer for the *Memphis*

Commercial-Appeal, wrote of the pairing, "It wasn't really a competition, but on this evening Randy Travis and Alan Jackson finished almost in a dead heat." Kerry Hill commented in the *Wisconsin State Journal,* "Tell George there won't be any empty footwear left behind"—a reference to "Who's Gonna Fill Their Shoes," the George Jones song that posed the question of who would walk in the footsteps of country's Hall of Famers.

Alan and Randy were quick to unite as songwriting buddies, cowriting the smash hits "Better Class of Losers," "I'd Surrender All," and "Forever Together." Of the latter, Randy recalls, "I started it on a piece of fax paper on a plane. Alan and I finished it on the bus." His insights into the nature of the relationship include the following details: "Every day we'd both go to the gym—he plays racquetball, and I lift weights—and then he'd come over to the bus, and Lib (Randy's wife and manager, Lib Hatcher) would fix us something to eat. We'd eat and then, if we had a writing appointment, we'd write until time to do sound check."

The union was an important one for both artists. Randy proved that he could write as well as sing, and he served notice that New Country hotshots such as Clint, Garth, and yes, Alan weren't going to blast him off the charts. Alan established he was a songwriter whom other singers could tap for material, and he has since contributed songs to the repertories of Faith Hill ("I Can't Do That Anymore"), Clay Walker ("If I Could Make a Livin'," which went to No. 1), and Chely Wright ("Till I Was Loved by You").

> You have a lifetime to write the first album, and a year to write the next one. It's hard sometimes to come up with a lot of personal experiences in the one year for that second album.
>
> —ALAN JACKSON

Spring brought the release of a new Alan Jackson album, *Don't Rock the Jukebox*. It was as much of an eye-opening sensation as *Here in the Real World* had been. Alan had a hand in writing nine of the ten songs, including all of the singles except "Love's Got a Hold on You." All the singles went to No. 1 on the *Billboard* chart except "Midnight in Montgomery," which stalled at No. 3 despite being the most powerful tune on the album. *Don't Rock the Jukebox* reached the second spot on the *Billboard* country album chart.

The first single to hit the airwaves was the title track. It would climb to No. 1, becoming Alan's second straight chart-topper. There's an interesting tale behind the origin of "Don't Rock the Jukebox." Alan and the Strayhorns were jamming at Geraldine's, a small truck-stop lounge in Virginia. "It'd been a long night," Alan recounted in a press release, "so I took a break and walked over to the jukebox. Roger Wills, my bass player, was already over there reading the records. I leaned up on the corner of it and one of the legs was broken off— and the jukebox was kind of wobbling around. Roger looked at me and said . . ."

Alan, Keith Stegall, and Roger Murrah got together in the interim between albums one and two and fleshed out the song. Alan had a notebook filled with lyrics and hooks. He let Keith peruse the notebook, and Keith picked "Don't Rock the Jukebox" as a musical sketch worth developing. The video for "Don't Rock the Jukebox" featured Hal Smith, who played town drunk Otis in *The Andy Griffith Show*, which Alan ranks as his favorite TV program.

Alan debuted "Don't Rock the Jukebox" in April on the Academy of Country Music Awards show. The performance went well enough, but something else happened that caused some amusement and embarrassment. A nominee for Top New Male Vocalist, the usually shy Alan became all too outgoing when announced as the winner. His acceptance speech started off wittily, as he jokingly thanked Garth Brooks for not being in the running. (Alan had four nominations, but the one for Top New Male Vocalist was the only one that didn't put him in direct competition with Garth.)

From that point, Alan's speech spiraled into a filibustering monologue. At the side of the stage, producer Dick Clark tried to get Alan to cut it short. The audience giggled, and the director bolted to a commercial while Alan was in mid-sentence. Why did it happen? Well, for one thing, Alan had grown used to telling longish stories between songs during his shows. He was also nervous, standing up there in front of his peers and millions of television viewers. The messages on the monitors, urging him to get it over with, went unseen because his eyes were locked on the folks in front of him. An unnamed source quoted in the *Akron Beacon Journal* said, "I don't think he had any idea how long he was on camera. He was really shocked when he came off and everybody was laughing about how much he talked."

No doubt Alan felt a little foolish when he found out about the gaffe, but truth be told, it was just an example of what a real (as opposed to show business) person he'd remained. He still had the capacity to catch stage fright and look silly in front of a crowd. Alan's lack of polish is part of what made him a true-blue man of the people, a superstar who could honestly say, "I still feel like the same guy who was driving a forklift in the Kmart warehouse ten years ago."

At least he had the chance to make a speech at the ACM Awards. A few months later at the Country Music Association ceremonies, Alan failed to win even one of the six categories in which he was nominated. That made him an unfortunate 0-for-10 in two tries at the CMAs. "I'm too new for some of the bigger awards, and too big for some of the newcomer awards," he surmised, taking the shutout in stride.

Any pain was eased significantly by the results of the fan-voted TNN/Music City News Awards, which in truth meant a lot more to Alan. In 1990 he had taken home Song of the Year ("Here in the Real World"), and in 1991 he was selected as Star of Tomorrow, with *Here in the Real World* being a carryover choice for Album of the Year. Alan's popularity with fans would continue to rise throughout the decade: 1992 brought a trio of TNN/MCN trophies, 1993 three more—including the coveted Entertainer of the Year. If those weren't the most meaningful moments of Alan's career, they were second only to his induction into the Grand Ole Opry.

An invitation to join the Opry is one of the clearest indications that a country musician has made it, and in 1991 that honor was bestowed on Alan. Becoming a member of the Grand Ole Opry is the fulfillment of a goal that most Nashville artists consider the loftiest that can be achieved. In his induction speech, Alan commented, "The ultimate dream when you're in country music is to be asked to join the Grand Ole Opry. It's the cornerstone of country music. . . . I'm proud to be a part of it."

Standing in "the circle" (the wood cutout from the old Ryman Auditorium stage that was transplanted to the stage at the new Opry House), the feeling is, according to Alan, hard to describe. Asked what comes to mind when he's standing in the circle, Alan explained, "You think about people like Hank Williams, who stood on that spot of wood, and Mr. Acuff, and, of course, George Jones."

One of the neat moments on *Don't Rock the Jukebox* is "Just Playin' Possum," a song Alan wrote in honor of his friend Mr. Jones. Alan and George share a mutual admiration: George has a bumper sticker that proclaims he's a fan of Alan Jackson, and Alan has one that lets folks know how he feels about the Possum. In late April 1991, Alan told the *Witchita Eagle*, "The friendship started about this time last year, when I kinda took off. . . . We just see each other a good bit when we're in town together."

Alan has also done a couple of duets with Jones: "I Don't Need Your Rockin' Chair" on *Walls Can Fall* and "A Good Year for the Roses" on *The Bradley Barn Sessions*. The Possum also rates a mention in "Don't Rock the Jukebox." Asked once what he thought was the main difference between being Alan Jackson in '91 and being George Jones in '58, Alan replied, "I think back then if you were a big star, you were still playing the honky-tonks and small state fairs."

> He's a nice man. He's a legend.
> —ALAN JACKSON on George Jones

Alan still had a long road to walk before he could be called a legend, but he was already represented in the Country Music Hall of Fame. It turned out that the wooden-box GE radio that Alan sang about in his hit "Chasin' That Neon Rainbow" was still around, and the hall wanted it for their collection. "We found it in my daddy's old garage," Alan remembers, "all greasy and nasty. That's the way they wanted it: just like it was. We didn't even wipe it off. We just brought it to Nashville. . . . My mom and daddy got a big kick out of it."

Ruth and Eugene were having the time of their lives, watching Alan succeed beyond their wildest dreams. Mrs. Jackson reported receiving "hundreds of letters and gifts" from fans all over the U.S., and she was tickled pink when Alan began copublishing songs under Mattie Ruth Musick, his mom's maiden name. "It makes me wonder if life really does slow down in retirement when I think of my name on a million records," Ruth gushed to an *Atlanta Journal-Constitution* staff reporter. "We figured some travel in retirement but we never thought we'd travel to Nashville as much as we do to see Alan sing at the Grand Ole Opry."

Eugene and Ruth had several chances to sit on the onstage wooden pews, which date back to the days when the Ryman Auditorium was a church, that are reserved for the close friends and family members of the artists. One of Alan's appearances at the venerable institution was more special than the others. On the sixty-fifth anniversary of the Opry, he performed as part of a television special. Alan commented, "The Grand Ole Opry, to a lot of people, is old-time, but to me, Nashville wouldn't be what it is if it weren't for the Grand Ole Opry.... I think that'll be something that I'll always remember."

By the time 1991 was said and done, it was clear that Alan would be remembered, too. *Radio & Records* picked him as the year's best overall new artist, and *Billboard* tabbed "Don't Rock the Jukebox" as the year's top country hit. One thing that sets Alan apart as an artist is that he's almost as good a writer as he is a singer. It's a fact the professionals recognized, and in 1991 Alan was selected the year's best songwriter/artist by the Nashville Songwriters Association International.

That honor came on the heels of a 1990 MCN Country Songwriters award for Song of the Year ("Here in the Real World"). It preceded an ASCAP award for Song of the Year ("Don't Rock the Jukebox.") In short, Alan was getting credit for being a creative force behind the hits, not just a great voice and a handsome face. He is a very rare Nashville animal: an artist who is as respected for his songwriting as for his work in front of the microphone.

"Every song's different," Alan explained in the *Roanoke Times & World-News.* "I've had songs come to me in three minutes and I've had some that have taken three years to write." Acknowledging that the well might one day run dry, he added, "Performing is where I started. Even when my songwriting burns out, hopefully I will still be able to sing."

"This good ole boy from Georgia is,
plain and simple, the real deal."
—David Sowd, *Akron Beacon Journal*

Classic Country: George Jones and Alan Jackson

Smile when you say *redneck*: Comedian Jeff Foxworthy finds a kindred spirit in Alan Jackson

First Families of Country: Alan and wife Denise with Mr. and Mrs. Randy Travis

Alan and Tammy Wynette

Kickin' back: Alan Jackson gettin' a little R&R

The Jackson family with special addition "Otis" from *The Andy Griffith Show*

Alan displays his 1993 Music City News Awards for Best Entertainer, Best Male Vocalist, and Song of the Year ("Chattahoochee")

A long, cool drink of water

Alan and Denise with George Strait and his wife,
Norma, at the ASCAP Country Awards dinner
in 1995

The winning spirit: Alan Jackson and Alison
Krauss at the 1995 CMA Awards. Alison won in
every category she was entered in; Alan won
Entertainer of the Year.

Alan with George Jones at the TNN Songwriter
Awards Show, 1994

Alan with Billy
Dean at the 1992
ASCAP Awards
dinner

Alan at Fanfair, 1992

Alan Jackson: a
true country star

SEVEN

Move on Up

He's got a new style with a traditional flavor,
but I think what makes him so popular is
the sincerity that comes through in his songs.
—LINDA LOU SCHRIVER, WXRL-FM, 1992

The success curve of Alan's career was tracking upward with no end in sight, and 1992 was to be his biggest year yet. The centerpiece: his third album, *A Lot About Livin' (And a Little 'Bout Love)*. It spawned five Top 5 singles, one of which turned out to be his biggest to date, "Chatahoochee." Writing in the *All Music Guide to Country*, critic Brian Mansfield enthused, "By this third album—when many artists start to run out of ideas—Jackson sounds like he's just starting to hit his stride."

A Lot About Livin' was set for release in winter; in fact, "Chatahoochee" didn't reach the charts until the following summer. Meanwhile, the opening months of 1992 belonged to *Don't Rock the Jukebox*, which was still selling well. The singles

"Dallas," "Midnight in Montgomery," and "Love's Got a Hold on You" were bound for the upper reaches of the *Billboard* charts.

Of "Dallas," Alan remembered, "We were down in Dallas playing Billy Bob's. The crowd was great—really excited. We'd never had a reaction like that. We finally had to pack it up and on the way back we were all saying how we wished Dallas was in Tennessee when we got home." Alan jotted the line in his notebook and later turned it into a song of heartbreak over a woman called Dallas.

"Midnight in Montgomery" was the fourth single from *Don't Rock the Jukebox,* and even though it didn't achieve the status of a *Billboard* No. 1, it was a top choice among critics and one of the dramatic highlights of Alan's stage show. Darker and more textured than most of Alan's compositions, "Midnight" is an homage to the glorious spirit and tragic life of Hank Williams Sr., who lived fast, died young, and left a legacy of musical genius that will never be diminished.

Alan and cowriter Don Sampson made a pilgrimage to Hank's gravesite. "The time I went was late at night and real stormy, and it was scary to be up there," Alan recalled. "I just sort of wrote from that experience. If you're a big fan of Hank's, and you go to that grave, you can feel weird about being there." The song hit *Billboard* No. 3 in May

1992, but it is a clear No. 1 in the minds of Alan's listeners. A critic in the *Buffalo News* once asserted, "If I had to pick one song that summed up Jackson's strengths as a singer and songwriter it would be 'Midnight in Montgomery.'"

April is the month when the Academy of Country Music honors its best and brightest. As was often the case during this period, the big winner was Garth, who took the trophies for Male Vocalist and Entertainer of the Year. But until the final fifteen minutes of the program, the night's standout was Alan, whose *Don't Rock the Jukebox* was chosen Single and Album of the Year by the three-thousand-member ACM. Accepting his trophies, Alan testified, "Thank God and the Grand Ole Opry for country music."

Alan's victory in the Album category was unexpected. Most folks figured a win for Garth's groundbreaking *Ropin' the Wind* album was a foregone conclusion. Alan confirmed in a *Los Angeles Times* interview that Album of the Year was "the award that was most surprising to everybody, including myself." Backstage at the Universal Amphitheatre, a disappointed Garth reportedly said to Alan, "That's the one I really wanted." Alan answered, "Well, I'm glad to have it too."

Alan's next awards experience came in June at

the fan-selected TNN/Music City News Country Awards. It had to be strange for Alan, hosting a gala sponsored in part by his former employers at TNN, where he was "really just the office gofer" during his first year in Nashville. "What makes me uncomfortable is people I used to work for, like the bosses," Alan later confided. "You still feel a little like you're supposed to be their employee or something."

This time, he was not only more than an employee, he was more than a nominee; in fact, Alan cohosted the festivities with Tanya Tucker. Those who weren't familiar with Alan's talkative side questioned whether he was the right man for the job. TNN director of programming Paul Corbin commented, "We taped a special with Alan in Austin, and I saw some sides to him that I hadn't seen before. . . . I think everyone will be pleasantly surprised."

In addition to cohosting the event, Alan led the nominations parade with a half dozen. The winners were chosen by the thousands of fans who phoned a 900 number to vote, with the proceeds going to various charities. When the calls were counted, Alan won in a trifecta of categories: Best Male Artist, Best Single, and Best Album (*Don't Rock the Jukebox*). After the ceremonies, Alan and his parents celebrated in classic fashion. "Well, that night my folks were in town, and we were all tired," Alan confessed. "I had a glass of milk and corn bread and went to bed."

A month or so after the TNN/MCN show, the Nashville Network aired its special on Alan, *One Night in Austin.* The premise was simple: Alan and his band playing live, with proceeds going to the PBS series *Austin City Limits.* At a video press conference not long after the taping, Alan answered questions from a roomful of national press critics. Asked whether he thought young fans might prefer a Garth-style stage show to his easygoing approach, Alan said, "I have as many young fans as any other kind, and they're the ones down front screaming and hollering. I don't think they feel like they're missing out on anything."

When asked how much overdubbing the special's producers had done, Alan answered, "We tried not to do anything that wasn't normal, and we didn't fix that much. Most people do a live show and then go in and redo everything so there's nothing left live except the crowd hollering. We didn't. We patched a few obvious things, but I believe if you're going to do a live show let it be as live as possible."

In mid-August the CMA announced its 1992 award nominees, and Alan's name came up four times: Song ("Don't Rock the Jukebox"), Video ("Midnight in Montgomery"), Entertainer, and Male Vocalist of the Year. That same week, a milestone event occurred at the Erie County Fair in upstate New York. Alan shared a concert bill with George Jones as the opener. "This is too much," the starstruck headliner told reporter Anthony Violanti. It was a rare case of a legend warming up for a red-hot newcomer. Concert critic Jim Santella pointed out, "The two country music traditionalists passed each other on the rocky road to stardom, headed in opposite directions." But he concluded, "In retrospect, it was a great night for country ghosts, past and present."

Considering the awards, the hit singles, the platinum albums, and the sold-out concerts, this was a period of incredible growth in Alan's career. But it wasn't just Alan: All of Nashville was riding high on the insurgence of new fans and new artists. According to a 1993 report on media and markets, country radio's penetration into the eighteen-plus age bracket reached an all-time high in 1992, then jumped another 5 percent the following year. The largest increase in young listenership was in the New England states, which are notorious for being the least receptive to country music.

The surge in public acceptance brought a rise in

media awareness, which meant a lot of reporters who were new to country suddenly were covering the Nashville beat. "They all ask, 'Why do you think country music's doing so well?'," Alan said. "I tell them that as far as I can see there hasn't been a change in the music. What I do musically is basically the same thing Hank Williams did forty years ago . . . just higher-tech production."

Alan sensed that the tough part might be behind him, as far as generating momentum was concerned. "It's rolling a little easier now than it was a year ago as far as the pressure of keeping it going," Alan revealed to critic Richard Cromelin. That said, Alan wasn't ready to relax just yet. "The way country music is growing," he noted, "it's a constant challenge to be creative or come up with the great songs."

I have this dog that listens to tapes with me, and if he barks at a song, I don't record it.
—ALAN JACKSON

Alan sure seemed up to the challenge of creating great songs—whatever it took. The final release from *Don't Rock the Jukebox*, "Love's Got a Hold on You," was on its way to the top slot on *Billboard*'s country singles chart. Alan was headlining a double bill with Diamond Rio, and his stage presentation featured a huge video system that gave folks in the back rows an upclose view of each bead of sweat on their favorite singer's brow. It was the same system used at the 1992 Grammy Awards and on pop star Paula Abdul's tour.

Some wondered whether it was going to be a sellout onstage, not just at the ticket booth, but those fears were unfounded. Alan wasn't about to start showing off, letting the video screens wag the artist. He was simply his usual unassuming self—cool under the spotlight. In truth, his subtle stage persona was enhanced by the fact that he didn't need to swing from a rope to make an impression on the folks sitting in the cheap seats. And his fans were totally into it. "Jackson was the only act to deliver the state fair two sellouts this year," said Ed Rock of the West Virginia State Fair.

As the summer of 1992 came to a close, Alan Jackson was as hot as hot gets. The one dark side was that he couldn't be at home. "It's hard," Alan lamented. "This week, [Mattie] fell and broke her arm, and it was difficult for me not to be there." On the first of October, Arista released "She's Got the Rhythm (And I've Got the Blues)" from Alan's third album, *A Lot About Livin' (And a Little 'Bout Love)*.

It's really a song with an R&B feel that Randy Travis and I wrote when we were on tour together. We had this bright idea to write something that wasn't quite so country because we wanted to pitch it to B. B. King. But I ended up taking it, arranging it, and making it my own.
—ALAN JACKSON on "She's Got the Rhythm"

As his first album had sold one million copies and his second effort two million, there were high expectations for *A Lot About Livin'*. Alan assured fans there'd be little departure from the sound they loved, telling Dean Rhodes of the *Phoenix Gazette*, "It's pretty much the same style. A couple songs are different. I wrote or cowrote most of them, but there's a few more outside songs. I think there's three this time around."

Alan debuted "She's Got the Rhythm" at the 1992 CMA Awards, but the focus was still on *Don't Rock the Jukebox*, which was at the end of its run as Alan's latest release. Of the four awards for which Alan was nominated, his chances in the Entertainer and Male Vocalist categories were considered slim, but he was in the thick of the scrum for the Song and Video prizes. When all the envelopes had been torn open, Alan was holding the Video of the Year award for "Midnight in Montgomery." It was his first CMA success in fourteen nominations, and although the Video award may lack the prestige of the Single, Song, Entertainer, and Vocalist prizes, at least Alan's CMA shutout was broken.

If he was just another hat act in 1989, Alan had carved a niche of his own by the end of 1992. The term *hat act* had entered the media vocabulary around 1987, when Ricky Van Shelton came on the scene. Since then it had been applied to Garth, Clint, Mark Chesnutt, and Alan, among others. Of course, none of the singers on whom that tag had been slapped were fond of it, and Alan was no exception.

In fact, Alan first donned a hat to conceal an L-shaped confluence of scars above his left eye. The two connected scars are from two childhood incidents. The first came about when one of his sisters tripped him as he was running through the house, causing him to crack his forehead on the coffee table. The second came when he crashed through a glass storm door while in the midst of playing a prank on one of his sisters. (Alan's intent, revealed in a *Country America* interview, was to give her a shock with a car part.

"You know, a condenser comes out of the distributor, and when it's charged up, it'll knock the fire out of you.")

His understandable attempt to cover up a prominent scar had led to his being lumped in with the hat-act club. He'd worked hard to get the dismissive label off his back. "I think everyone's gotten tired of hearing it," he was quoted in the *Greensboro News & Record*. "Me, I've worn a hat onstage for ten years." He rang in again on the subject later, asking, in effect, what he was supposed to wear. "It goes hand in hand with the music I do."

Sticking to his guns, being himself, just plugging along, Alan had made the most of his decade in the spotlight. *A Lot About Livin'* had shipped 750,000 units by December and was bound for a million by Christmas. Alan had been on the road for at least 180 concert dates and a plethora of other public appearances in 1992, and he was going to be just as busy in the coming year.

EIGHT

Year to Remember

I don't think I've changed all that much
from a kid who grew up in a small town.
—ALAN JACKSON

Alan earned the title *superstar* in 1992, and his hard work in 1993 solidified his position as one of the hottest names in Nashville. From the rise of "Chatahoochee" to his personal-best seven CMA nominations to the birth of his new baby daughter, it was to be a memorable year in the life of Alan Jackson.

"She's Got the Rhythm" had peaked at *Billboard* No. 1 the final week of October '92, making it the sixth of Alan's past seven singles to reach the top spot. The second release from *A Lot About Livin'* (and the first of 1993) was "Tonight I Climbed the Wall," a heartfelt ballad that hit *Billboard* No. 4 in late February. Alan feels strongly about the ballads he writes, and he insists, "Whether they're sad or not, that's the real stuff." Many of Alan's listeners feel the same, evidenced by the *Entertainment*

Weekly writer who enthused, "Jackson's songs crackle with succinct character sketches and vibrant language."

While his songs rode the radio airwaves, Alan was touring in a turquoise bus bearing a destination sign that read REAL WORLD, which signified not only his first hit single but the places and people Alan counts on to help keep his head on straight. "I've really got the best of both worlds," Alan told Michael Corcoran of the *Dallas Morning News*. "Every night I get to be ALAN JACKSON, the one they've paid their money to see, then afterward, I can go get a hamburger somewhere . . ."

One advantage of being on the bus was that it afforded Alan a chance to concentrate on his songwriting. The demands of the road were forcing him to focus less on the crafting of new songs, which in some respects wasn't such a bad thing. "I got into this songwriting thing out of necessity more than anything else," Alan has said. Being a bestselling artist in a town full of professional songwriters, he no longer felt the pressure to crank out an entire album of songs on his own. Nashville is the songwriting capital of the world, and Alan was flooded with pitches from the best in the business.

On the other hand, he didn't like to stray too far

from the path that had taken him to the top of the charts, and contributing to the writing process was a part of that path. Except in rare cases, such as his recent album of tributes to the great honky-tonk tunes of the past, Alan's name has been among the writing credits on all of his releases. For a reluctant songwriter in a town packed with gung-ho scribes, Alan is still one of the aces in his field.

> To me, songwriting is the backbone of Nashville. Looks can go, fads can go, but a good song lasts forever.
>
> —ALAN JACKSON

In addition to being the one place on the road where Alan could set his mind to writing songs, the tour bus was the place to kick back and relax. A favorite pastime among the band members was listening to soundboard tapes of infamous performances by famous artists. The most notorious such tape is perhaps the one of Linda McCartney singing an amusingly off-key version of "Hey Jude," which the crowd never heard but the soundman isolated and saved.

Another classic is the recording of Hank
Williams Jr. playing in Kansas City one night after
falling off the wagon. Poor ol' hammered
Bocephus manages to sing just one line of "All My
Rowdy Friends" (the band plays numerous
impromptu solos to pass the time). He curses,
sings out of tune, and collapses after less than half
an hour onstage and is carried away as the band
plays on. "Well, you can bet they'll never forget
that show," Alan commented in a *Dallas Morning
News* interview.

Alan can appreciate the overindulgence that has
been the calling card for most of his musical
heroes, but he isn't itching to fill their shoes in
that regard. In contrast to the missteps of, say,
Merle Haggard—who once wound up in prison
because he was too drunk to notice that the joint
he was breaking into was still open—Alan's learn-
ing experiences have been more like those of a
Horatio Alger character.

Alan's songs seem to present a pretty accurate
reflection of his attitudes about life. He tries to
keep things positive, and doesn't dwell on his
mistakes. He's actually an old-fashioned romantic. Once a reporter asked him, "But what about
all those old drinkin' and cheatin' songs? Isn't
that what country music was all about?" Alan
asserted, "Like almost any other musical format,

it's about love most of the time."

In another interview, Alan explained that his littlest listeners inspire him to keep his nose clean: "There are so many young fans, some just children, who idolize you, and you really have to be careful about what kind of image you're sending out to them." Maybe because he has small children of his own, Alan is extremely conscious of setting a good example for kids who look up to him. "In fact, most of our fan mail is from little kids. I see some in the audiences who can't stay awake long enough to hear 'Don't Rock the Jukebox.'"

Alan's amazing music touches all types of listeners—male, female, old, young, rural, urban, and in between. His songs are always honest and never fall short of inspiring, whether it's the ballads or the shuffles, the lighthearted or the serious ones. That's why you'll hear them in a high-schooler's pickup or a soccer mom's minivan, at the grocery store, at the ballpark, or in the bedroom. When you get down to it, there is nothing more universal than a country song, and nobody who does one quite like Alan.

> He's really the same shy, gentle, but very strong-willed person that he was in the beginning.
>
> —TIM DUBOIS

Alan's career had chugged through and past the *Don't Rock the Jukebox* stage, but the fans who singled out the winners of the 1993 TNN/Music City News Awards were still in the process of recognizing the work he'd done on his second album. Alan walked away with Male Artist of the Year, Entertainer of the Year, and Video of the Year ("Midnight in Montgomery"), a haul of trophies that could be interpreted as a landslide election for the most popular man in country music.

You know an artist is in the zone when folks are still talking about his last album even as his new one is shooting up the charts with a bullet. That was the case leading into summer 1993, arguably the hottest stretch of months of Alan's career to date. He kicked off June in St. Paul performing at the Civic Center with one of his idols, Merle Haggard.

In the meantime, Alan's sensational new single "Chattahoochee"—complete with a video featuring Alan hanging loose on the lake in his custom-made red boots—was being hailed as a season-defining anthem. On June 12, the single cracked the top of the *Billboard* chart, where it remained for an impressive four weeks. "It's a song about having fun, growing up and coming of age in a small town," Alan mentioned in a press release.

It was just a simple little ditty—albeit one with an opening guitar riff that sticks in your head and never leaves—but it made an awful lot of commotion at the cash register. "We never thought it would be as big as it's become," Alan was heard to say. "Chattahoochee" was soon certified gold.

The Country Music Association hit Alan with a personal-best seven nominations and a trio of awards: Single and Video of the Year for "Chatahoochee," plus Vocal Event of the Year for his part in the George Jones hit "I Don't Need Your Rockin' Chair" (with Vince Gill, Mark Chesnutt, Garth Brooks, Travis Tritt, Joe Diffie, Pam Tillis, T. Graham Brown, Clint Black, and Patty Loveless).

Unfortunately, the Academy of Country Music couldn't find its way clear to honor Alan with one award, bestowing its coveted trophies on Garth Brooks and Vince Gill. But a lot of the problem with the 1993 ACMs had to do with timing—the Academy covered *Don't Rock the Jukebox* the previous year and would honor *A Lot About Livin'* at the following year's ceremonies.

> Look at George Strait. He's never been somebody who wins everything, and he's no flash in the pan. Yet everybody likes him and is still pulling for him. I'd like to be thought of in the same way.
> —ALAN JACKSON

But there were observers who felt Alan had gotten shortchanged again by the CMA, despite the two wins. He had yet to be chosen as either Entertainer or Male Vocalist of the Year, those being the two most coveted prizes offered, but he wasn't about to moan about it himself. "Oh, I usually win a little somethin' or other," he drawled to one reporter. When it was suggested that Alan's situation was parallel to that of Randy Travis years before, he offered, "We're too country. Too country for country."

Still, it's hard to feel cheated when the albums are flying off the store shelves and the fans are clamoring for more. With all that was going on in Alan's life, last but not least was the most important event of 1993: On August 23, all seven pounds, three ounces of Alexandra Jane Jackson came into the world. Although things weren't as hectic in Alan's life as they'd been when Mattie Denise entered the picture, he still wasn't able to spend as much time as he wanted to at home with the new baby. But her presence would be felt in his heart from the start, and more than ever, Alan found himself looking toward home when he was on the road.

And the road is exactly where he was as fall marched toward winter: touring the Western half of the U.S. with John Anderson ("Seminole Wind") as his opening act. Alan still had the two big screens, with intercutting shots of his video clips and the action onstage, and he still had a big inflatable jukebox that jiggled and bounced during "Don't Rock the Jukebox" (". . . like Barney reincarnated as a coin-op machine the size of a triceratops," wrote one critic.)

By the time October rolled around, Alan was well into promoting the fourth single from *A Lot About Livin'*, an up-tempo number known as "Mercury Blues," which would later be adapted for a commercial ("crazy 'bout a Ford truck"). It climbed as high as No. 2 on the *Billboard* chart, becoming the ninth single of Alan's career to reach that plateau.

It's somewhat strange that in the biggest year of his career, Alan didn't put out an album of original material. There just wasn't time—or for that matter, need. But he did manage to put together a special treat for his fans: the first and only Alan Jackson holiday album, appropriately titled *Honky Tonk Christmas*. Alan explained, "I wanted to find songs that sounded like my kind of country music, but Christmas-style." It was a neat twist on the typical holiday album, with the one recognizable classic in the collection being "Holly Jolly Christmas," a song that meant a lot to Alan. "I learned it as a kid," he has said, "and now I sing it to my daughter."

Other than that, *Honky Tonk Christmas* doesn't contain "Jingle Bells" or "Silent Night" or any of the favorites you'd expect. Instead, it features the likes of "Please Daddy (Don't Get Drunk This Christmas)," which Alan has called "a song I can hear some ol' bar band playin' late on a December night with everybody singin' along," and Merle Haggard's "If We Make It Through December," which Alan at first tried to alter to sound less like Merle, "but then it didn't sound right at all."

Honky Tonk Christmas also offers some tasty duets, including ones with bluegrass star Alison Krauss, cartoon heroes the Chipmunks, on whose Nashville album Alan had performed the previous year, and the late Keith Whitley, with whom Alan sang via an old demo. (The book *Definitive Country* notes that Alan also put out a holiday record in 1991, titled *I Only Want You for Christmas*, which made the Top 50 but is no longer in print.)

Not all of Arista and Alan's choices for singles made the five-pound-bass of a splash that, for example, "Chatahoochee" did. In fact, "Tropical Depression" barely rippled the Top 75, lasting only a week in that range before falling off radio programming lists.

To close out 1993, Alan released one last single from *A Lot About Livin'*, a song he has cited as one of the best he's ever written, the stirring ballad "(Who Says) You Can't Have It All." Alan explained in a press release, "I've always thought it was a classic country lyric and a real moving song." True, but it was, to an extent, a risk to come out with a slower-tempo single at a point when his momentum was up, particularly since his last slow single, "Tonight I Climbed the Wall," turned out to be the lowest-charting hit of his career.

Sadly, it can be tough to garner support from country radio for ballads, even though, as Alan stresses, "those are the songs that really affect people." For what it's worth, "(Who Says) You Can't Have It All" topped out exactly where "Tonight I

Climbed the Wall" had, at No. 4 on *Billboard*. But that didn't bother Alan, who isn't inclined to watch the charts or sales numbers, preferring instead to focus on the music and let the other stuff take care of itself.

NINE

King of Country

Alan is the current country king.
—BILL IVEY, director of the
Country Music Foundation, 1994

And boy was the "other stuff" ever taking care of itself. Alan's first two albums were still among the most popular back-catalog items in country music, and his third was approaching the three-million-sold milestone. About the time "(Who Says) You Can't Have It All" reached its chart peak, Alan was gearing up to release his first album of original material in too long. The fans had been patiently waiting to find out what Alan had under his hat, and as a matter of fact, it was his most intimate album yet: the soulful declaration he titled *Who I Am*.

Music journalist Brian Mansfield writes in the *All Music Guide to Country*: "In a time when even artists had trouble telling all the young hat acts apart, a personal statement like *Who I Am* was possibly the smartest move Jackson could have made." Even the symbolism of the cover art seemed significant; props are prominent on *Don't Rock the Jukebox* (vintage Wurlitzer) and *A Lot About Livin'* (vintage Harley), but on *Who I Am* the cover art is simply a nice closeup of Alan and his Stetson.

Of course, the music's the thing, and this was without doubt the most consistent release Alan had yet produced. Sure, the singles were terrific, but more than on previous albums, the supporting tracks were strong enough to keep listeners hooked from start to end. Non-singles such as "Job Description," in which Alan tries to explain to his daughters why their daddy is gone so long and so often, and "Let's Get Back to Me and You," wherein Alan addresses the toll that can be taken on a neglected marriage, are some of the best songs.

Another gripping ballad is "Hole in the Wall," cowritten with Jim McBride. Alan recalls, "We pictured this guy who had lost his loved one, and when she left him, he took her picture off the wall and left a hole there that was just eating away at him." It sounds on *Who I Am* as if Alan cranked up the personal aspect of his songwriting, and he confirmed, "Overall, the new songs are probably closer to the real me." And it's worth noting that there are thirteen tracks, a nice break from the

Nashville standard of ten, although the thirteen songs on *Who I Am* are numbered one through fourteen, owing to Alan's confessed superstitious streak.

"Jackson's smooth baritone, reminiscent of the fifties, is suspended between moaning fiddles and crisp snares," wrote reviewer David Zimmerman to describe the sound of *Who I Am* and Alan's sound in general. That was in sharp contrast to the lavish trappings of his concerts. All told there were thirty-nine tons of equipment involved in his stage production, hauled around in tractor trailers, buses, a merchandise truck, and a mobile home for the caterer.

It was a little odd when you thought of it: this basically shy guy whose music evokes a simpler time and basic truths, surrounded by all this big money and expensive gear, electronic flash onstage and questions re his underpants offstage, and on and on ad infinitum. But the cool thing was that he never let the superfluous stuff dictate. It was Alan's show, and he always set the tone—no matter what went on around him.

On the first night of his 1994 tour, at the Sunrise Musical Theater in Miami, F-L-A, Alan was smooth and easy, and the crowd was with him each and every step of the way, through all the time-tested favorites—"Wanted," "Working Class

Hero," "Midnight in Montgomery," and "Chasin' That Neon Rainbow"—as well as new material such as "Mercury Blues." As one critic succinctly put it, "He's not a flashy performer—no rhinestones on his shirt, no exaggerations in his voice—and he doesn't need to be."

> Jackson is one of the few artists in today's prepackaged, glittery world of country music who ignores the flash, the pretenses and the industry schmoozing. Yet he's still as hot as fresh-baked biscuits.
> —MARIO TARRADELL, *Miami Herald*

You can find plenty of commentary along such lines in the critical consensus of mid-nineties Nashville. Alan and his fellows from the Class of '89 had, for the largest part, gotten beyond the hat-act label (which implied that they were clones and possibly phonies), but the next generation of male country artists was considered a generic lot by many of the same people who dismissed Alan, Clint, Garth, et al. at the beginning of the decade.

Actually, even Alan was heard to comment, "When I listen to the radio, the songs and the artists are getting harder to tell apart." Alan also told a *Journal of Country Music* writer, "There's some good stuff out there, but it seems like everything now is slide guitars and Hammond organs," meaning not the traditional instrumentation of straight-up stone country.

In such an atmosphere it's usually best to either stick with what made you recognizable in the first place or do something radically different from anything done before. Alan chose to do both in the first single from *Who I Am*. Back in 1958, the year Alan was born, a visionary named Eddie Cochran wrote and recorded an anthem called "Summertime Blues." It hit only No. 8 on the pop charts, but it's now considered an absolute classic.

Years later, the song was brought back in hard-rock form by Blue Cheer, a 1960s group credited in the *Rolling Stone Album Guide* for being "bad taste of an almost surreal intensity" (the band, not the song). This is the version that most people know, and it's doubtful that anyone ever expected to hear it covered by a country singer in 1994 (although Buck Owens had tried it at some point). Yet that is what Alan decided to make happen, at the urging of Keith Stegall.

It was a stroke of brilliance in that Alan was able to throw listeners a changeup—"What the heck is this? Hey, I know that song!"—but still give them his own signature sound and feel.

Incorporating an opening guitar line that mirrors "Chattahoochee" was also smart and effective. It was not much of a coincidence that one year after "Chattahoochee" hit No. 1 in *Billboard*—give or take a couple of weeks—"Summertime Blues" busted the exact same move. "I can relate to the 'Summertime Blues,'" Alan said in a press release, "because growing up in Newnan . . . we always lived for the weekends."

One could get the impression Alan was experiencing some personal blues in the early months of 1994. He seemed intent on making big changes—and little ones, too. He shaved the mustache he'd worn for thirteen years, but Denise insisted he grow it back. Then he grew a beard, saying "it seemed like the thing to do in the wintertime." He later told the *San Antonio Express-News*, "Every time I grow something or cut something off, I get lots of comments from people."

Of course, these minor alterations might not have been indications of a larger, brewing dissatisfaction, but coincidence or not, in March 1994 Alan made a major change, severing ties with his manager, Barry Coburn. Although no one except Alan will ever know the reasons, it's been speculated that the flash point was an incident that occurred when Alan was set to perform on an album of duets with George Jones.

The Possum was scheduled to sing with several Nashville standouts, all peers of Alan's. On the morning he was scheduled to record, Alan got wind that the prize in a radio contest was a chance to visit the studio and hear the session. Alan called Barry, concerned that the studio would be a mob scene, and Barry called the producer to suggest setting up security. It wasn't such an unreasonable chain of events, but somehow impressions got twisted so that Alan came off looking like a prima donna in some people's eyes. Soon after, Alan fired his manager.

Barry spoke extensively on the subject in Laurence Leamer's book *Three Chords and the Truth*, asserting that he was the one person who wasn't afraid to disagree with Alan and give him a motivational push: "I was the guy that was saying, 'Well, I don't agree with you on that, I think you need to write better songs,'" Barry recalled. "I was the one that forced him to write songs. I mean, I used to threaten to put people on the bus to write with him unless he wrote, and people he didn't like, mind you. That was the only way I could get him to write songs."

On the possible reasoning behind Alan's decision, Barry explained to Leamer, "I think he probably felt that he had reached the point in life where he didn't want anyone telling him what to do or anyone criticizing him. And I was the only one that would. If I felt that the show wasn't that good and he was really just lazy on a particular night—and he wasn't like that very often—but if I saw a bad show, I'd tell him. I never held back. I'd say, 'I thought that was pretty bad. I think you could have done a lot better there. You weren't really communicating.' And he'd go, 'Oh.'"

In the short term after Barry's departure, Alan still seemed intent on reprioritizing his life and career. He made the decision to sell the rights to his entire song catalog for a hefty thirteen million dollars, which was reportedly a record for a Nashville writer, blowing away the three-million-dollar deal Merle Haggard had signed the year before. "I really don't know how many of today's artists are going to have the staying power of a Willie Nelson or a Merle Haggard, but Alan will," said Donna Hilley, the head of Sony Tree Music Publishing. "Thirty years from now those songs will turn over again and be recorded by new artists—songs like 'Here in the Real World' and 'Don't Rock the Jukebox.'"

Another development in 1994 was the inauguration of the annual Center Hill Lake concert, dubbed Boatstock. It seems Alan's most treasured Fourth of July memories are of taking a boat out onto the local lake. "There were hundreds of boats out there at night to watch the fireworks and I always just loved that," he reminisced. Alan later concluded that if ever given the opportunity, he'd put on a show designed just for recreational boaters.

So on a late-July weeknight, underneath a blazing spotlight that naturally attracted every flying insect within range, Alan played and sang for two hours on a stage set twelve feet above the water on a peninsula at Edgar Evins State Park for a flotilla of boats that numbered in the thousands. Everyone managed to have a good time without anyone getting into trouble, but a few intrepid souls tried diving in for a swim to the front of the stage before being gently turned back.

The concert was held at Alan's expense, and he brought his own boat, *Neon Rainbow*, to help check water depths with the U.S. Corps of Engineers earlier in the week. These were some of the same people who'd helped him arrange filming of the "Chattahoochee" video on Old Hickory Lake near Nashville, and Alan wound up signing on to be the National Water Safety Spokesman for the following year.

The concert has since become a greatly anticipated semiannual happening, drawing up to tens of thousands of music and boat lovers, based on aerial photographs. Unfortunately, the 1998 show didn't come off as planned. "It was unbelievable, like flipping a light switch," said Ed Carter of the Tennessee Wildlife Resources Agency, commenting on the thunderstorm that forced the cancellation of the concert. Eight of the smaller boats sank, and many others were swamped by the sudden bad weather.

The inaugural 1994 concert served as the kickoff to the next leg of a tour that took him and the crew west. It was too bad that all his shows couldn't be at dockside, but while he wasn't in a position to take to the water and go boating at every stop along the circuit, Alan did maintain a trailer of motorcycles to ride in his spare time. "One thing about getting out on a Harley-Davidson, riding it out in the country, is that nobody can see you, nobody can call you, nobody can talk to you." Not that he had a lot of free time, what with the demands of the media and the fans and his managers, not to mention all of the preparations—sound checks and such—required to pull off Alan's stage production.

On the other hand, that stage production was so elaborate—and thus totally managed—it kept Alan from needing to get tied up in the comings and goings. "This ain't a proper job," he confessed.

"Sometimes all I have to do is turn up; everything else has been done." When he hit the stage, though, it was clear that none of the ostentation— the cameras panning up his legs to his tush, the footage of a sexy female dancer during "She's Got the Rhythm"—would mean a thing if not for Alan's innate charm and his honest music.

That balance, which was also evident in the mix of songs—for instance, stir up a whole lotta fun with "Chattahoochee" or "Summertime Blues," and add a dash of drama with "Midnight in Montgomery" or a bluegrass-gospel rendition of "What Kind of Man"—keeps Alan's concerts from being either too staid or too superficial. It's the essence of just about everything Alan does: a balance between apparent contradictions that, in the final result, comes out just right.

Yet another admirable aspect of Alan's concerts is the practically limitless age range of the audiences. You'll find everyone from great-grandparents to toddlers singing and clapping along with Alan and the Strayhorns. *Orange County Register* reporter Gene Harbrecht once commented, "That's a real tribute to Jackson's ability to produce a style of country that almost perfectly blends tradition with a sensitivity to contemporary interests."

No wonder Alan was one of the top three

country artists of 1994 in total concert receipts, running neck and neck with Reba McEntire, following only Garth.

TEN

Back to Basics

He alone represents almost 50 percent
of the sales of Arista-Nashville.
Believe me, folks, I love this man.
—TIM DUBOIS

The first week of September, the people at
Arista threw a wingding for Alan in celebration of
his eleven million albums sold. The breakdown
went something like this: two million for *Here in
the Real World*, three million for *Don't Rock the
Jukebox*, and four million for *A Lot About Livin'
(And a Little 'Bout Love)*. On top of all that, the
Honky Tonk Christmas album was certified at a
cool 500,000 copies sold, while *Who I Am* was at
1.5 million and counting fast. Not too shabby for
a late-starting career that was a mere four years
old.

Following his characteristically sheepish acceptance of the commemorative plaques, he told the
audience, "This is a party, drink up and be somebody, I guess." Soon after, he came up to the

115

microphone and announced that instead of doing his usual solo acoustic show, he would invite various cowriters to join him in doing their songs. Some of the artists who took him up on the offer were Don Sampson, Keith Stegall, Jim McBride, and Zack Turner.

Before "(Who Says) You Can't Have It All," which he'd written with McBride, Alan told the audience, "I had to fight to get it on our album, and I even pitched it to George Jones, and he didn't get it on his album. Now, this is real country music, people." With regard to that subject, Alan didn't stop there. He went on to dryly add that, in the wake of compilations such as *Common Thread: The Songs of the Eagles*, McBride and Jackson had considered putting together an album with the unique concept *Country Artists Do Country Music*.

In addition to being a deserved honoring of Alan's accomplishments, the Arista shindig was an excuse to remind CMA voters to think of Alan when the time came to choose their Male Vocalist and Entertainer of the Year for 1994. He'd already scored the awards for Single and Album of the Year from the Academy of Country Music, and cohosted the awards show as well. (The ACMs are awarded in the spring and cover the previous year, hence the victories for 1993's *A*

Lot About Livin' and "Chattahoochee.")

Alan had also been the biggest winner at the TNN/MCN Awards, taking the trophies for Male Vocalist *and* Entertainer—not to mention prizes for Single and Video ("Chattahoochee"), and Album (*A Lot About Livin'*). But again, that was primarily for nominations related to *A Lot About Livin'*, whereas the 1994 CMAs covered both *Who I Am*, nominated for Album, and *A Lot About Livin'*, from which "Chatahoochee" was up for Song. Alan was also in the running for Entertainer and Male Vocalist.

When the envelopes were opened, Alan was holding a pair of 1994 CMA Awards: one for Song of the Year, which was shared with cowriter Jim McBride, and one for Album of the Year, which was shared with the other artists who had performed on the *Common Thread* compilation. Vince Gill went home with both the Entertainer and Male Vocalist trophies, while Alan went back on the road.

At the Worcester Centrum near the end of October, his show sold out in two hours. A writer for the *Boston Globe* called it "a startling feat by any standard," and claimed Alan was "hotter than Garth Brooks"—a tired comparison but a nevertheless useful measure: There were few singers in the genre who could warrant the praise. But in this case it wasn't a stretch; Alan's fan base was huge—and getting bigger all the time.

He spoke to reporter Steve Morse about the difference between the salad days when he appeared strictly in small venues and the jelly days, in which packed arenas were the rule: "Even though I'm fairly new to this business, since I've come along, it's easier for an act to come out with just one record and one video and all of a sudden they're a star. It's not like when I was starting out."

In the second half of 1994, Alan put out two singles from *Who I Am* that would've made him a star under any circumstances. First came the infectiously hummable "Livin' on Love," a song that Alan proclaimed "sounds just like my mama and daddy's life." It zoomed to No. 1 in late September and still holds up as one of the most requested songs on Young Country radio.

In a press release, Alan talked about how, in spite of the fact that he wasn't thinking of them when he wrote it, the song reminds him of his parents. "They married when they were kids and all they ever had was each other and their family. Now they're at the age where all their children have grown up and gone, and they still sit on the front porch swing, just like the song says."

Alan followed "Livin' on Love" with what is arguably his best-known song outside the general parameters of country listenership: the scathingly sarcastic "Gone Country," which was later adapted to "Ford Country" for a pickup-truck commercial. Its original form is the ultimate jab in the ribs to people who flock to Nashville when there is money to be made, although Alan downplayed the hard truth by explaining "Gone Country" as "just a fun song actually, celebrating how country music has become more widespread and accepted by all types of people all over the country." Alan did note that there are an awful lot of musicians in Nashville whose true hearts lie in a genre other than country, be it southern rock or the blues or folk music or classic rock or bubblegum pop. In that light, he did confess to being "scared that country music's losing its identity a little bit."

Alan was doing all he could to keep the identity strong and clear, at least in his own life. In mid-February 1995 he and the Strayhorns pulled into Montgomery, Alabama, to perform in concert, then perform a ritual they'd established for all their trips to the city where the body of Hank Williams rests.

A long time before, following a late-night pilgrimage to Hank's grave, Alan had written "Midnight in Montgomery" as a tribute. Since then, every excursion he made to Montgomery included a trip to the graveyard and a midnight acoustic jam. Enough fans were aware of the ritual that police had to cordon off the area so Alan and his band could reach their destination.

The musicians bring guitars and perform their favorite Hank songs, plus the most heartfelt "Midnight in Montgomery" imaginable. Moments such as those go to the soul of what Alan Jackson the artist is all about. Not that he doesn't get a kick out of cutting loose with a full electric band in front of thousands of cheering fans, but it's still the intimate settings and acoustic classics that inspire him most.

On the winter's evening in question, the party was treated to a mystical moment. Alan told *Chicago Tribune* writer Jack Hurst, "As we were going through the song we looked over, and there was this falling star that was real bright. . . . And when we got to the end of the song where I stop and make a little pause there before I say the last line or two, you could hear a train way off in the background blowing its horn."

It was pretty weird, like Hank was saying hi
or something.
—ALAN JACKSON

Alan's first single of 1995 was a gem of an affir-
mation about keeping in touch with the things in
life that matter most, like sunrises and children,
laughter and love. "Song for the Life," one of the
few Alan hits he didn't write himself, was inked by
Rodney Crowell, who credits Alan with steering
him back toward traditional country and away
from the pop and rock influences he'd been
under. The song was particularly meaningful to
Alan because he had come the full route: from
having little in the way of material possessions to
having everything he could want to realizing that
what counts in life is not the stuff you get but the
love you give and receive.

Alan's next single (his eleventh *Billboard* No. 1)
was the tongue-in-cheek song "I Don't Even
Know Your Name." The story behind the hit is
that every time Alan and Denise went to Newnan
to visit her older brother, he and his stepson
would tell Alan they had a song idea for him: "I'm
in love with you, baby, and I don't even know your
name." It was an ongoing joke between them, but

years later Alan was on tour in the Northwest and decided to flesh out the concept. He and the Strayhorns then made a recording for his brother-in-law. "The next thing I know," Alan explains, "everybody that hears it starts commenting how cool it is and how they really like it."

That was the fourth and final release off *Who I Am*, an album that yielded two flat-out classics and a whole bunch of enduring music. An interesting thing had happened when the album was released: Although a majority of critics praised the work, there were some who wondered aloud if Alan was losing his touch. If those doubters were members of the Academy of Country Music, they must have been in the minority, because 1995 was the year that Alan brought home one of the Academy's most sought-after trophies—the Male Vocalist of the Year award.

Certainly there were no doubters among the fans who phoned to vote for the TNN/MCN Awards. Just as he'd done the year before, Alan won Single of the Year ("Livin' on Love"), Album of the Year (*Who I Am*), Entertainer of the Year, and Male Vocalist of the Year—an incredible sweep of the four crucial categories in which he was eligible. Also just as in 1994, in 1995 Alan tossed in a fifth TNN/MCN, this time for a collaboration with his friend George Jones on "A Good Year for the Roses."

While you'd hardly call 1995 his biggest year in an artistic sense, you'd have to think of it as a kind of convergence of recognition. The fans had spoken loud and clear for two straight years, the Academy of Country Music had seen fit to honor Alan as its best Male Vocalist, and the press was trumpeting him as the savior of traditional country music. Many felt it was time for Alan to get his due from the Country Music Association.

Alan was nominated in six categories: Album (*Who I Am*), Single ("Gone Country"), Vocal Event ("A Good Year for the Roses"), Video ("I Don't Even Know Your Name"), Male Vocalist, and, of course, Entertainer—the one everyone was rooting for Alan to win. Alan waited the entire evening to hear his name called—sitting through Alison Krauss's four wins in four events and Vince Gill's fifth straight Male Vocalist title—but when the moment came it was worth it. When the presenter, Johnny Cash, announced the winner of the 1995 CMA Entertainer of the Year, the name he called was Alan's.

Clutching an antique penknife that once belonged to Hank Williams and was given to Alan by Marty Stuart as a good-luck charm, Alan graciously accepted the honor. Afterward the proud performer declared, "I went from playing truck-stop lounges several years ago to doing it for fifty thousand people at the Houston Astrodome. I feel qualified [to win]." It was a rare instance of self-acknowledgment by a man once described as "pathologically averse to giving himself any but the most minor credit."

Back on the road, Alan was touring with an up-and-coming singer named Faith Hill, who every country fan now knows as one of the best female vocalists in Nashville. While it's true that Alan has written several hits for other artists, he rarely sits down to pen a tune with a specific person in mind. Yet when Faith playfully joked that Alan should write a song for her to sing, he went to his bus and did it.

As a matter of fact, he wrote two. First he composed a song, meant to be sung by a woman, called "It's Time You Learned About Goodbye." As he told a *Chicago Tribune* writer, "Good song . . . But [Faith] said, 'That's a little bit more country than what I'm doing' or something like that." Alan had to be a little disappointed to hear such a sentiment, especially from an artist whose vocal talents are so perfectly suited for straight country, but he headed right back to the drawing board.

Alan said, "Well, I'll just go write another one," but this go-round he decided to "write something that wasn't very country." The song he created, "I

Can't Do That Anymore," was never released as a single, but it is arguably the most poignant song Faith has ever recorded. It is interesting to note that there was a measure of disagreement between Alan and Faith over the line about the washing machine. He wrote it to say that the character dreamed she was a washing machine, but Faith chose to sing that she dreamed *about* one. Alan tried to no avail to explain. "The way I wrote it didn't literally mean a Maytag. It just meant this woman was a machine around the house."

Some folks, including Faith, speculated that the song might have been written with Denise in mind. Alan confirmed that, while she never suffered to the extent of the character in the song, Denise had made sacrifices for his career and for the good of their relationship. It hadn't gotten easier to be a star's wife. "Alan and I try to have a normal family routine," Denise told Wendy Newcomer. "Get home, do homework, play outside, cook supper, eat supper together. It's mainly making sure that everybody else is away so that we can have one-on-one time with our girls."

For his part, Alan long ago came to the understanding that he had to do whatever it took to be at home as much as possible. Being the best father and husband he could was a paramount concern. It helps that Alan truly loves his family and is at heart a born romantic. "He's the kind of guy who, if you're at the lake, wants you to hurry up eating so you can go up on the deck and watch the sunset," Denise revealed.

> Country music is a long, tall, golden-haired Southerner with a smooth Georgia drawl and a knack for telling rich musical stories of simple people going about the complicated business of life.
>
> —GENE HARBRECHT,
> *Orange County Register*

For his '95 tour, Alan chose to tone down the visual aspect of his stage show, flattening the stage by lowering or eliminating the risers. He also went back to using amplifiers rather than earphones for monitors, which affects how "live" the musicians sound to one another. "I just think that you can lose what you came from and it gets to where it's just a show and not music anymore," Alan explained. As he told Michael Miller of the *Columbia State*, "I've been looking back at the production part of my show and realized that it's been getting bigger every year—more lights, more video, more staging. I started wondering where all this was going."

Even after Alan's setup was scaled back, it still took a corporate sponsor—in this case, Fruit of the Loom—to foot the bill. And the underwear folks went so far as to make Alan the centerpiece of their 1995 promotional efforts. It was a perfect match for both parties, except that Alan was pressed to answer about a thousand inquiries concerning whether he'd don a pair of tighty-whities for the camera. The answers were along these lines: "I'd have to go on a training course for a few months before I could do that. I don't think anybody wants to see me in my Fruit of the Looms."

One result of the cleaner, leaner stage setting was better reviews and even greater fan support. Vickie Gilmer of the *St. Paul Pioneer Press* raved that Alan's "surefire blend of heart-wrenching ballads and barroom rousers won over a crowd of 21,278." Many of Alan's shows were so intensely anticipated that the seating areas behind the stage sold out.

From comments made by Alan and his manager, Gary Overton, it wasn't hard to figure out who their role models were. "George Strait goes out there with just ten lights in the air and a microphone stand," enthused Gary. For his part, Alan noted that "[Merle Haggard's] just as cool as ice, you know. He walks out there and stands in his place, and he doesn't even know what he's going to be playing. He just starts banging on that ol' Telecaster and singing whatever comes to mind." Alan expressed a similar admiration for Waylon Jennings, who, when asked how he prepares for a gig, fired off one of Alan's favorite quotes: "Well, I just get off of whatever it is I'm sitting on and walk out there and sing."

Despite lightening his load onstage, Alan wasn't about to give up on-the-road comforts like his chuck wagon. To feed his entourage of fifty-plus folks, a catering crew of five followed the tour in a mobile home that towed a kitchen trailer, cooking recipes supplied by Alan's wife and his mother. That meant plenty of homemade favorites, including pineapple and mayonnaise sandwiches on white bread, with chips or pork 'n' beans from a can. Not to mention all the corn bread, fried okra, and country-fried steak a man and his friends could handle, finished off with chocolate meringue pie for dessert.

Back to Basics

> When we go through Georgia, we stop at my folks' and Mom cooks for us. [The Strayhorns] really like the soufflé. It has sugar and butter.
>
> —ALAN JACKSON

During a gig at Starwood Amphitheatre in Nashville, October 1995, Alan let the fans in on a little secret: "I'd like to warn you that the next album is a package of greatest hits, songs we've been singing here tonight." It was hard to imagine that just five years before, Alan's first Arista album was bursting onto the scene. Now he was issuing a greatest-hits collection.

It was a revelation worth savoring, and the packed house at Starwood did exactly that, from the opening lines of "Chasin' That Neon Rainbow" through the closing notes of "Mercury Blues," up until Alan doffed his hat and held up a pair of cowboy boots (a gift from an audience member), saying, "Y'all behave now, y'hear."

There were two tunes Alan sang on that chilly evening in Nashville that even his most dedicated fans didn't know: "I'll Try" and "Tall, Tall Trees," which were the two songs from *The Greatest Hits*

Collection that weren't previously available. Each would be put out as a single in the months to come, and both would hit No. 1 in *Billboard*. A third single, "Home," which was just an album track on *Here in the Real World*, climbed as high as No. 3.

The story behind "Tall, Tall Trees" is one of the most entertaining and representative of Alan's repertoire. It seems he found a cassette in a box of miscellaneous recordings. The tape was labeled simply ROGER MILLER SONG, and it contained a little slice of musical nirvana with a hint of Cajun spice. The recording was from an old vinyl LP— "just twin fiddles and a screechy sound," Alan says. "But it kept haunting me."

As it turned out, the song was cowritten by none other than the Possum himself, George Jones. That makes it extra special for Alan, who noted, "I think George had even forgotten he'd written it." And added, "I was a little afraid to do it, but when it came out on the radio, by God, it stood out, I guarantee you." The song held on to *Billboard*'s top spot for two weeks near the end of October, and spent a full nineteen in the Top 40.

ELEVEN

Keepin' the Pace

Not true. They weren't napkins.
They were paper towels.
—ALAN JACKSON's answer to the question of
whether it was true that he once carried a brown
bag full of napkins with scribbling on them into
Tim DuBois's office and announced, "Here are
the songs for my next album."

Alan kicked off 1996 with his thirteenth
Billboard No. 1, "I'll Try," a song he wrote about
commitment. Not a conventional "I'll stay with
you till the stars fall from the sky" wedding song,
it is, as Alan explained it, "a realistic approach to a
positive love song." On tour with Wade Hayes and
Tejano star Emilio, Alan blew audiences away with
his passionate renditions of "I'll Try."

During this time, Alan's stage show was more
potent than ever. The Strayhorns were at the peak
of their prowess, and Alan rewarded them night-
ly by reserving a spot on the song list for "Stray
Hornpipe," an instrumental from their own

album. The song list was smokin' in and of itself, with perfect portions of his *Greatest Hits Collection* classics, outtakes from his upcoming album, and raucous covers of all-time greats such as Hank Williams Jr.'s "Texas Women."

Alan also introduced his "half-wired" sets (so called due to the fact that, "even though it's acoustic, you've still got to plug in to be heard"), which featured shortened versions of older hits ("Wanted," "Here in the Real World"), songs he'd written that had been hits for other artists ("Better Class of Losers," "If I Could Make a Livin' "), and Alan's heart-stopping bluegrass rendition of the Eagles classic "Seven Bridges Road," complete with an acappella opening and closing.

If Saturday night's country music extravaganza at Atlanta Motor Speedway had been a road race, Alan Jackson would have lapped the field.
—RUSS DeVAULT,
Atlanta Journal-Constitution

Keepin' the Pace

Next up on the singles chart was a song from *Here in the Real World* that hadn't been put out as a single previously: "Home." It is one of Alan's most personal testimonials. He once revealed, "I wrote it when I was homesick. I've traveled a lot of places I thought I'd never be. . . . And one thing I find is that wherever you go, there's one place you call home." Alan intended to release the song as a single in 1990, but Joe Diffie just happened to do a tune of the same title, and by the time Joe's song finished its chart run, Alan had gone on to his next album.

There's no doubt that *The Greatest Hits Collection* is a must for Alan's longtime fans, as it's the disc that contains the essential "Trees," "Try," and "Home." It's also the best place for a newcomer to begin fostering an appreciation of Alan's amazing songwriting and singing. Those facts account for the album's chart success—it debuted at No. 1 on *Billboard*'s country album chart and at No. 5 among the Top 200 in all genres. All of Alan's albums continued to smash through the loftiest of sales levels: *A Lot About Livin'* stood at six million, *Don't Rock the Jukebox* cracked the four-million barrier, *Who I Am* touched the three-million plateau.

Through it all Alan came across as one cool customer, taking it all in stride. "Every day you sit and talk about yourself in interviews, and people tell you how great you are," he observed. "Nobody wants to make you mad. Every now and then I get grumpy and think I'm too good, but my wife will kick me in the rear." If he were prone to getting a swelled head, Alan sure would've needed a boot in the pants after the Academy of Country Music selected him Male Vocalist of the Year for the second year in a row.

A couple of months later, Alan was at the TNN/MCN Awards to pick up trophies for Male Artist of the Year (his fifth straight) and Entertainer of the Year (fourth straight). Alan was thrilled, of course, but on the awards front, those would have to hold him for the remainder of the year. Despite receiving four nominations for 1996 CMA Awards—Male Vocalist and Entertainer, plus Video and Vocal Event (both for "Redneck Games," a collaboration with Jeff Foxworthy)— Alan was left out of the winner's circle.

Summer of '96 was filled with good times and nostalgia. In late spring, an ad appeared in the Newnan classifieds, offering a residence for sale that was billed as "formerly Alan Jackson's home." Around that same time, his beloved '55 Thunderbird was on display near Newnan at the Pigs 'n' Wheels Bar-B-Q Cook-off and Car

Show. It seemed like there were little pieces of Alan all over the place.

So it was fitting that he would be back in Newnan for the Fourth of July. Alan served as the grand marshal for Newnan's Independence Day parade, riding in back of a vintage Chevy Impala with the superintendent of schools at the wheel. Later in the evening, Alan performed a short concert for a packed grandstand before being escorted home in the county sheriff's car.

> That's the way I like it: people who still know who they are.
> —ALAN JACKSON

It had been quite a while since Alan had put out a new album of all original material, but in 1996 he and Keith Stegall flew down to the Florida Keys, where Alan has a house and a boat. The two songwriters spent a couple of days fishing and listening to demo tapes. Keith brought some Harley Allen recordings, and he thought there were a couple of songs that might be right for Alan.

"Between the Devil and Me" was one that made the cut. Keith later said in *Country Weekly,* "I felt like 'Devil' might be a stretch, but I thought that it was something that once he sang it, it would sound like a country record, even as contemporary as it is." In the course of picking songs, there are usually some worthy prospects that get brushed aside.

One item from Alan's cardboard box of songs, "Way Beyond the Blue," has come close to making it onto an album several times. "I just love this old thing," Alan has said.

Asked how he chooses songs, Alan often jokes about following the advice of his dogs or playing rate-a-record with his wife and children. But there's actually a great deal of thought that goes into it, and most artists, Alan included, sift through a vast number of demos before settling on the half dozen or so that'll go on an album. The task is particularly daunting in Alan's case because he walks a line between pushing into new musical frontiers and keeping the familiar sound and feel his fans adore.

Part of the responsibility for maintaining that sound falls to Keith and the musicians he hires for Alan's studio endeavors. "The band on his records has become so much associated with his music that I keep those guys in mind every time we make a record," Keith once explained. "If I find songs that I know he can make believable, when you put that rhythm section around it, it comes out sounding like an Alan Jackson record."

Alan's fifth album of original material (his seventh if you include *Honky Tonk Christmas* and *The Greatest Hits Collection*, both of which contained some originals) was the exquisitely executed *Everything I Love*. It exhibits all of the growth and confidence gained from prior studio efforts, as well as inspired song selection. There are a pocketful of genuine jewels here: from obvious hits such as "Little Bitty" and "There Goes" to album tracks such as "It's Time You Learned About Goodbye" (the song Alan wrote for Faith Hill that she rejected).

> I've always had the suspicion that lots of people out there led perfectly contented lives, and didn't have any need to try and be Tom T. Hall—or Alan Jackson for that matter.
>
> —TOM T. HALL

Late in 1996, Alan released a cover of an obscure Tom T. Hall tune first heard on the album *Songs from Sopchoppy*. The song "Little Bitty" quickly sailed to the top of the *Billboard* chart—in fact, it got there quicker than any of Alan's singles ever had. The song is a brilliant blending of bouncy, catchy melodies and sharp insights into the essence of contentment.

Some listeners interpreted its presence on the album as a sign of Alan's dissatisfaction with the price fame exacted on his personal life— forcing him to live large when he still felt "little bitty" inside. But he dismissed such ideas, claiming, "I just thought it was a fun song that said a little something."

While he wasn't inclined to complain too much about the toll a public life can take, Alan was often confronted with situations that, while harmless enough in most respects, could grate on the nerves of a man like him. At one point in 1996 he was obligated to explain to his mom that, contrary to rumor, he hadn't purchased a small city in Florida. According to Jack Hurst of the *Chicago Tribune*, "Mama, I haven't bought a town," were Alan's words of reassurance to his puzzled mother.

Speaking of stories being blown way out of proportion, one was swirling around that Alan had signed a gal's bare backside at a Taco Bell in Murfreesboro. The disc jockeys at one radio station were bantering about it on the air, but Alan later set the record straight by explaining that he had indeed been at the spot in question (following a flying lesson, no less), when a big crowd of autograph seekers were asking him to sign whatever they could get their hands on. He asserted, however, that he didn't sign anyone's butt. "I ain't saying I wouldn't," Alan told Jack Hurst, "but I don't remember doing it that night. I was just trying to eat my burrito and get out of there."

In the earliest months of 1997, the press releases were flying fast and furious from the Nashville offices of Arista, as a stream of new events was flowing in Alan's life. First came the wonderful news that Denise was pregnant with their third child, expected in September. Their plan was to get a sonogram, and Alan stated, "We didn't want to know the sex of our first two, but we do on this one." He told an audience at the Wildhorse Saloon in Nashville, "From now on, you can call us the Jackson five!" Denise and Alan's third daughter, Dani Grace Jackson, was born on August 28.

> When my girls do something very small, it means something big to me. Just watching them accomplish things from the time they're infants is wonderful.
> —ALAN JACKSON

In spring Alan signed a deal to represent Ford trucks in a series of commercials that would center on modified versions of the songs "Mercury Blues" and "Gone Country." It seemed appropriate, as his dad had worked at Ford's Atlanta plant for twenty-five years before his retirement in 1989. In a speech he made at the Hapevillle facility's fiftieth anniversary party, Alan said of his father, "The money he made up here put a lot of gas in my go-cart."

Alan himself sold Fords for three years in the 1980s, and he made another sale after signing on as spokesman, when George Jones went to a dealer, bought himself a new F-350, and sent the company a note reading, "You can credit my friend Alan Jackson with his first sale."

Two other pieces of news were that Alan had amassed a stunning twenty-three million albums sold in his career, and that *Everything I Love* had achieved platinum status in March. With the royalties he was collecting, Alan could try new business endeavors, and in that spirit he announced he was breaking ground on a restaurant—the Alan Jackson Showcar Cafe—at a cost of more than five million dollars. Chip Peay, who'd been Alan's agent for over a year, noted, "This is a life-long dream for Alan."

It was destined to be another dream of a summer, as the single "Who's Cheating Who"—

backed by a video featuring Alan in a monster truck and cameos by NASCAR stars—was on its way up the charts. ("There Goes" had already climbed to No. 1.) Although he'd failed to win a thing at the spring ACM Awards, in June he took home his sixth consecutive TNN/MCN Award for Male Artist of the Year and his fifth consecutive Entertainer of the Year award. "Y'all are spoilin' me," Alan told the crowd.

August brought the unveiling of the 1997 nominees for the CMA Awards, with Alan in the running for Male Vocalist, Entertainer, and Album. In an interesting turn of events, just as Alan was shut out at the ACMs, while LeAnn Rimes won prizes for best single and best song, he would be blanked at the CMAs, where Deana Carter won in the single and song categories. As it happens, both LeAnn and Deana were among the new female artists who opened for Alan on his 1997 tour.

No doubt there was an infusion of fresh blood pumping through the veins of Nashville; a veritable women's revolution was under way. Yet there was still room for an old-fashioned honky-tonk survivor such as Alan Jackson, and as of late 1997 his sales totals looked like this: *A Lot About Livin'*, 6.5 million; *Don't Rock the Jukebox*, 4.5 million; *Who I Am*, 3.8 million; *The Greatest Hits Collection*, 3.5 million; *Here in the Real World*, 3 million; and *Everything I Love,* more than 2 million and counting.

"Alan Jackson and George Strait led the way in 1997," commented Lon Helton of the trade publication *Radio & Records,* which named Alan the year's Most Valuable Performer. *Billboard* also placed Alan at the head of the country class for 1997, based on his chart success.

TWELVE

Stayin' Together

We were like the Ken and Barbie
of country music, but it turned out
we had problems like everybody else.
—ALAN JACKSON

In winter 1998, at a time when he appeared to have it all going in his direction, Alan entered what had to be one of the most troubling times of his life. Reports that the Jacksons were enduring marital problems had been circulating around Nashville for weeks, and in February it was confirmed that they had separated after almost nineteen years of marriage.

A spokesperson for the couple, Nancy Russell, told the press, "It is a personal matter and we would appreciate everyone respecting the family's privacy." The request was respected for the most part, but Alan did vent a little about the media, saying with a laugh, "They've been trying to find some dirt on me for years to talk about. All the press wants to talk about is the bad stuff."

Alan's fans were on pins and needles waiting for news of the marriage's fate. Denise and Alan were talking things through, although Alan had performance obligations to fulfill. At a concert north of the border in Edmonton, a sore throat prevented him from doing a sound check until minutes before it was time to hit the stage. The ailment had forced the cancellation of his scheduled appearance in Saskatoon two nights before, and it appeared to reduce his energy in Edmonton.

There's no doubt Alan was under a lot of stress, and he needed to recharge. "I was going crazy, I guess," he later told Associated Press reporter Jim Patterson. In the midst of his separation from Denise, he took a solitary road trip through the Deep South. It was during this time of avoiding the interstates—visiting small towns and seeing their struggles for survival—that he started writing the lyrics to "Little Man," which would become the signature single from his upcoming album, *High Mileage*.

Some of the song choices for the album reflect a painful phase in Alan's life and career, with titles such as "Gone Crazy" and "Hurtin' Comes Easy" representing the blues Alan and Denise must've been suffering. When divorce seemed imminent, Alan went so far as to record a cover of REO

Speedwagon's classic rock song "Time for Me to Fly."

In a *Chicago Tribune* interview, Alan tried to put his finger on the source of the trouble, observing, "We got married as kids and didn't really know who we were, and kind of like a lot of people that have been married as long as we have . . . you're growing apart and you're living together and not liking each other: loving each other but not liking each other."

Of course, the great news, as everyone knows, is that Alan and Denise found the will to repair their sputtering marriage and get back on track—better than ever. Not surprising, the key was professional assistance, something that he had resisted. "I've never believed in counseling or therapy, and I didn't think I needed anybody to help me with my problems," he later stated. "But I finally gave up and went to get some good help this time—and I needed to."

Apparently that did the trick. The Peach Buzz section of the May 28 *Atlanta Journal-Constitution* crowed, "You heard it here first!" and passed along the news that Denise and Alan had reunited. Publicist Nancy Russell confirmed, "They are back together and we're all very happy up here." So were the fans, who wanted nothing more than for the Jacksons to work things out and rediscover the positives in their relationship. Denise later admitted, "This separation was the most devastating experience I have ever gone through. I couldn't imagine the possibility of being divorced from the only man I've ever loved."

In light of the new developments, it was appropriate that the first *High Mileage* single be the passionate paean to inner love and beauty, "I'll Go on Loving You." The song was unusual in several respects, both as a departure from Alan's established style and from what most of Young Country radio was playing. It is sensual, even a bit suggestive with its "as you slip off your dress" line, and the spoken-word aspect is uncommon. "There may be a stretch or two on [*High Mileage*] but nothing that takes me as far as 'I'll Go on Loving You' does," asserted Alan.

The tradition of "talking songs" dates at least to Hank Williams and his Luke the Drifter persona. Some others include Tex Ritter's "I Dreamed of a Hill-Billy Heaven," C. W. McCall's "Convoy," George Strait's "You Look So Good in Love," and the 1970 hit from Conway Twitty, "Hello Darlin'," which is definitive of the form. During a talk with TNN's Crook & Chase, Alan responded to the observation that recitations are hardly ever heard these days: Alan stated flatly, "Conway's dead.")

Alan's dry sense of humor also comes across in

a prank he pulled on the people who were filming the "I'll Go on Loving You" video. He secretly inserted a set of "Billy Bob" teeth before opening his mouth to speak the opening lines. The juxtaposition of ultraromantic lyrics and oversized-chompers brought on a veritable riot of laughter in the studio.

Alan and the people at Arista considered the possibility that radio wouldn't support "I'll Go on Loving You," but that didn't stop them. Senior Vice President of Marketing Fletcher Foster observed, "Obviously, it wasn't the most typical radio-friendly song that was on the album. . . . But we also knew that it was different, and that if it could catch on, it would be big." Alan believed people would identify with the song if given the chance to hear it. "I think it has a real sweet message," he said.

At the 1998 CMAs, Alan sang the last verse of "I'll Go on Loving You" in Spanish, and the audience reaction was overwhelming. (He later cut the Spanish version for radio stations in the Southwest and California, and requests poured in.) But the most talked-about aspect of the thirty-second CMA Awards in regard to Alan was his absence from the list of nominees.

It was an abrupt change for an artist who had been nominated for Entertainer of the Year each year since 1992 and for Male Vocalist of the Year each year since 1991. But much of the reason had to do with timing. Alan hadn't been very active during the period that the awards covered. "Believe me, I don't see this as any kind of a career problem," Fletcher Foster said. "A lot of it is the result of things like the timing of his album releases and his deciding to take a break from touring."

Be that as it may, Alan was also left out of the winner's loop at the 1998 ACMs, and, more disturbingly, the TNN/MCN Awards, which he had essentially dominated for the past five years. That didn't mean he wasn't still a major fan favorite; in fact, his fan club was said to be the largest in country music. "Hello, my name is Alan Jackson, and I'm a country music singer," he humbly introduced himself at his 1998 Fan Fair fan club party, the sweetest moment of which came when he covered "Together Again," a Buck Owens classic, to celebrate his reunion with Denise. Alan brought her and their girls on stage at the Ryman Auditorium to the delight of the thousands of lucky and loyal fans.

Despite being shut out at the three major awards ceremonies, Alan did get to stand at the winner's podium for something that a scant few Nashville singers ever do. For the third time in his career (the first two being in 1993 and 1994), Alan was chosen Songwriter of the Year by the American Society of Composers, Authors, and Publishers. The gala was held at the Opryland Hotel, and in attendance were the likes of Vince Gill, Trisha Yearwood, Brooks & Dunn, Bryan White, and Trace Adkins.

Probably a hit song about a marlin!
—ALAN JACKSON when asked if he'd prefer writing a hit song or having a marlin on the end of his fishing line

---

High Mileage was pretty well received in the cramped, crabby circle of critics. The praise ranged from mild ("A good effort") to medium ("For those with an ear for traditional country, Jackson's latest is a no-risk disc") to hot ("As a beacon of excellence in unsettled musical times, Alan Jackson's continuing triumph proves that quality can win"). Record reviewers didn't universally embrace "I'll Go on Loving You"—one commented "Julio Iglesias in a cowboy hat"—but they adored "Little Man" and "Right on the Money," both of which went on to become No. 1 hits.

As for Denise and Alan's relationship, it felt brand new, especially after they renewed their wedding vows on their nineteenth anniversary in December. "I see that separation as a gift," she was quoted in *Life* magazine. "It forced us to put our attention back on our relationship." But she also added, "If any of my three girls even *mentions* marriage before they're thirty, I'm gonna lock them up." Alan seemed to feel the same way about both the relationship and the subject of young marriage in general.

Alan also had an opinion about the hard row that new artists have to hoe, and he had a plan for making it easier. Recalling the times he was allowed to open for established stars such as Alabama and Randy Travis, Alan decided to model his High Mileage Tour after the old Opry road shows of the fifties. "I thought this would be a good idea, seeing as it's so hard to get a leg up in this business," Alan commented. The rotating procession of artists opening for Alan in the first half of 1999 included Chad Brock, Sara Evans, and Clint Daniels.

FOURTEEN

Pure Tradition

Somebody told me the album needs
to come with a six-pack of beer.
—ALAN JACKSON

In the opening days of the new century, there is a pervading sense that the Nashville of 2000 may be even worse than the one of 1980—just as watered-down and with fewer distinguishable personalities. That's why Alan's decision to do an album that mines honky-tonk tradition for its material was such a stroke of inspiration. *Under the Influence*, consisting exclusively of covers, is arguably the most important country album of the year.

If it seems strange that an artist who is so admired for his songwriting would "stoop" to recording an album of nothing but nonoriginals, consider that Alan is, above all else, a country music *fan*. He has a superb collection of classic recordings, and his song repertoire includes a bunch of the all-time, old-time hits. He's been

151

playing and singing some of them (and others in a similar vein) since his days of performing in bars and nightclubs. While the collection spans eighteen years, seven of the songs are from a brief span (1979–81) when Alan was stepping onto small stages and singing for small crowds.

The idea was perfectly simple. Get some good buddies—each of whom happens to be a crack instrumentalist—in a recording studio to pick and sing on tunes such as "Pop a Top," the barroom shuffle that Jim Ed Brown made a big hit in 1967; Gene Watson's tragicomic ballad "Farewell Party"; and "Revenoor Man," which George Jones first sang when Alan was but five years old. It's an amusing coincidence (or is it?) that *Under the Influence* starts with "Pop a Top" and ends with Jimmy Buffett's "Margaritaville."

Alan reports that the Possum was one of the first people on the planet to hear the album. "I ran into him the other day," Alan relates, "and he was just going on and on about it. That made me feel great, because I wanted to make this album as a kind of tribute to those artists." It's for that reason that Alan decided to play all the songs as close to their original version as possible, rather than try to put his stamp on the songs.

That said, one of Alan's most rewarding qualities as a musician is his knack for making the old sound somehow fresh and infusing the new with a feeling of tradition. It's a talent that keeps *Under the Influence* from coming across as a mere novelty or nostalgia. Several of the selections are so obscure and rarely heard that these versions will become *the* versions for any fan who isn't a country music historian. But that shouldn't be a problem, since Alan has stuck close to the true intent of the original artists.

Probably the most recognizable of the compositions is Charley Pride's "Kiss an Angel Good Mornin', " which Alan tabs as "a great sing-along song that makes people feel good." The most out-there pick of the litter might be "The Blues Man," a Hank Williams Sr. jewel that was never a single. It's autobiographical, about Hank and one of his wives, and Alan simply changed the "I" to "he." There are two Merle Haggard songs, two George Jones ditties, and a pair of tunes penned by Bob McDill, the man who wrote Alan's smash "Gone Country."

Under the Influence seems destined to go down as a classic itself, but there's no telling what Alan will do next, what turns his career will take. You can bet his fans will be behind him all the way, and that Nashville is going to look back in years to come and say, "Thank God for Alan Jackson." Meanwhile Alan will be spending time with his wife and daughters, working on his boats and cars, wettin' a hook and riding the waves, and making music for as long as it feels like it should. As he once let it be known, "When the fun goes, so will I."

```
┌─────────────────────────────────────┐
│  ┌───────────────────────────────┐  │
│  │                               │  │
│  │         Alan On...            │  │
│  │                               │  │
│  └───────────────────────────────┘  │
└─────────────────────────────────────┘
```

Songwriting

"Basically, I'm lazy. What little writing I get done, I do on the road."

Stardom

"The people that work for me call me a hermit. I just don't really like the star part of the business."

"I wish when I get off the bus I could be more normal and go down to Kmart and buy me a fishing lure."

"You spend your life workin' for it, and I know there's folks who'd trade with me any day, but there are still things I miss."

Touring

"The hardest part of this job is to try to explain to a three-year-old girl why I have to be gone for several days."

155

Gary Cooper and Jimmy Stewart

"They came from rural backgrounds, and all of them went into World War II. . . . They had lived, and they were real people when they walked onto the screen."

His Legacy

"I don't know that I'll ever impact people the way George Jones or Hank Williams have. If anything, I hope I'm keeping a little bit of traditional country music alive for the next generation so they'll know what it is."

Marrying Young

"I've watched and witnessed so many people who get married young, like I did, and their situations change, and they change, and the people around them change. And sometimes they make a commitment, 'I will' or 'I do,' and then it ain't the same five years later, and it doesn't work."

Working When He's Older

"I think most people like to cut back a little when they get older. I think a lot of people keep working because they have to, not because they're enjoying it as much. If George Jones had been a little more careful in a business sense . . . he might have quit twenty years ago."

Alan on . . .

Priorities

"It's my family and love that's real important to me. I guess probably the toughest goal to set now is just being a good husband and father."

Fixer-uppers

"I've always loved buying something that's wore-out and making it look new again."

Keeping It Real

"I come from little bitty. My pocketbook's a little bigger, but my heart's still that way."

Fishing

"I'm not really as serious a fisherman as people make me out to be. I just love the water. That's why I got into fishing, but I do enjoy the thrill of catching a fish. . . . You go out fifty miles in the Gulf of Mexico and there's not a soul in sight. . . . It's just calm and beautiful."

Hunting

"I've never been a fan of hunting. Probably never will be. We had a .22 rifle, which we kept in the house, but that was all. It was never in my blood and I never want it to be. I'll go fishing, but most of the time I'll throw back what I catch or I'll eat it. I don't really believe in killing for the sake of it."

APPENDIX I

Personal Data

> And if anyone can learn about the music
> business from the mailroom at TNN, they're
> a lot smarter than I am.
> —ALAN JACKSON

Name: Alan Eugene Jackson
Born: October 17, 1958
Birthplace: Newnan, Georgia
Parents: Eugene and Mattie Ruth (Musick)
Siblings: Older sisters Diane, twins Cathy and
      Carol, and Connie
Education: Graduated from Newnan High
      School (1976); attended West Georgia
      Community College
Current Residence: Brentwood, Tennessee
Marital Status: Married Denise Jackson
      December 15, 1979
Children (Born): Mattie Denise (6/19/90);
      Alexandria "Ali" Jane (8/23/93);
      Dani Grace (8/28/97)
Hair: Blond
Eyes: Blue

APPENDIX I

Voice: Baritone
Height/Weight: 6'4" / 180 lbs.
Guitar: Jim Triggs
Hat: Stetson Silver Belly
Former Jobs: Forklift operator at Kmart;
    mailroom worker at TNN
Hobbies: Collects classic cars, antique boats,
    and Harley-Davidson motorcycles
Favorite Sports: Fishing, water-skiing
Favorite Foods: Brunswick stew; pineapple
    and mayonnaise sandwich
Favorite Film: *The Outlaw Josey Wales*
Favorite TV Show: *The Andy Griffith Show*
Influences: George Jones, Hank Williams,
    Merle Haggard, Gene Watson
Favorite Songs (from *The New Country Music
    Encyclopedia*): "He Stopped Loving Her
    Today" (George Jones), "Rose Colored
    Glasses" (John Conlee), "Are the Good
    Times Really Over for Good," "The
    Grand Tour," and "Farewell Party"
    (Gene Watson)
Three Words That Best Describe Me (from the
    Chicago Tribune): Old-fashioned,
    romantic, ignorant
One Thing I Can't Stand (from the *Chicago
    Tribune*): Cigarette smoke in the
    morning

The Strayhorns (High Mileage Tour):
- Monty Parkey (piano, harmonies)
- Robbie Flint (steel guitar)
- Danny Groah (lead guitar)
- Bruce Rutherford (drums, harmonies)
- Tom Rutledge (acoustic guitar, banjo)
- Tony Stephens (harmonica)
- Roger Wills (bass)
- Cheryl Wolff (fiddle, harmonies)

Alan Jackson International Fan Club:
- P.O. Box 121945
- Nashville, TN 37212-1945

APPENDIX II

Discography

The younger fans don't care what it is.
They don't put labels on the music.
—ALAN JACKSON

Albums

Here in the Real World, 1990
Don't Rock the Jukebox, 1991
I Only Want You for Christmas, 1991
A Lot About Livin' (And a Little 'Bout Love),
     1992
Honky Tonk Christmas, 1993
Who I Am, 1994
The Greatest Hits Collection, 1995
Everything I Love, 1996
High Mileage, 1998
Under the Influence, 1999

Duets and Compilations

George Jones: The Bradley Barn Sessions, "A
     Good Year for the Roses" with George
     Jones

Walls Can Fall, "I Don't Need Your Rockin'
      Chair" with George Jones and others
Keith Whitley: A Tribute Album, "Don't Close
      Your Eyes" with Keith Whitley
Mama's Hungry Eyes: A Merle Haggard
      Tribute Album, "Trying Not to Love You"
Redneck Games, "Redneck Games" with
      Jeff Foxworthy
Common Thread: The Songs of the Eagles,
      "Tequila Sunrise"
Star of Wonder: A Country Christmas
      Collection, "Rudolph the Red-Nosed
      Reindeer"

Videos

Here in the Reel World, 1990
Livin', Lovin', and Rockin' That Jukebox, 1993
The Greatest Hits Video Collection, 1995

APPENDIX III

Awards and Honors

Of all the things I've done, places I've been,
and awards I've won, I still get more excited
when I sit on the bus and write a good song.
—ALAN JACKSON

Academy of Country Music (ACM) Awards

1990 Top New Male Vocalist
1991 Single Record of the Year, "Don't Rock
       the Jukebox"
1991 Album of the Year, *Don't Rock the
       Jukebox*
1993 Single Record of the Year,
       "Chattahoochee"
1993 Album of the Year, *A Lot About Livin'
       (And a Little 'Bout Love)*
1994 Male Vocalist of the Year
1995 Male Vocalist of the Year

Country Music Association (CMA) Awards

1992 Music Video of the Year, "Midnight in
       Montgomery"

1993 Single of the Year, "Chattahoochee"

1993 Music Video of the Year,
   "Chattahoochee"

1993 Vocal Event of the Year, "I Don't Need
   Your Rockin' Chair" with George Jones

1994 Song of the Year, "Chattahoochee"

1994 Album of the Year, *Common Thread: The
   Songs of the Eagles*

1995 Entertainer of the Year

TNN/Music City News Awards

1990 Song of the Year, "Here in the Real World"

1991 Album of the Year, *Here in the Real
   World*

1991 Star of Tomorrow

1992 Male Artist of the Year

1992 Album of the Year, *Don't Rock the
   Jukebox*

1992 Single of the Year, "Don't Rock the
   Jukebox"

1993 Male Artist of the Year

1993 Entertainer of the Year

1993 Video of the Year, "Midnight in
   Montgomery"

1994 Single of the Year, "Chattahoochee"

1994 Video of the Year, "Chattahoochee"

1994 Album of the Year, *A Lot About Livin'
   (And a Little 'Bout Love)*

1994 Male Artist of the Year
1994 Entertainer of the Year
1995 Single of the Year, "Livin' on Love"
1995 Vocal Collaboration of the Year, "A Good
        Year for the Roses" with George Jones
1995 Album of the Year, *Who I Am*
1995 Male Artist of the Year
1995 Entertainer of the Year
1996 Male Artist of the Year
1996 Entertainer of the Year
1997 Male Artist of the Year
1997 Entertainer of the Year